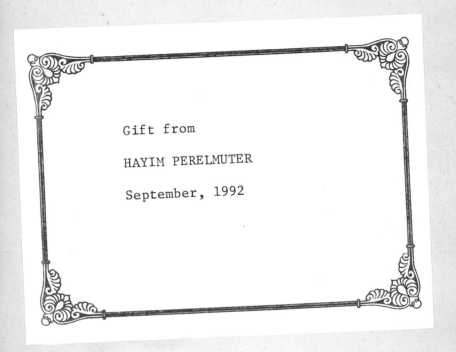

Gift from

HAYIM PERELMUTER

September, 1992

BY-PATHS
IN HEBRAIC BOOKLAND

BY-PATHS
IN HEBRAIC BOOKLAND

BY

ISRAEL ABRAHAMS, D. D., M. A.

Author of "Jewish Life in the Middle Ages," "Chapters on
Jewish Literature," etc.

PHILADELPHIA
THE JEWISH PUBLICATION SOCIETY OF AMERICA
1920

PREFACE

Wayfarers sometimes use by-paths because the highways are closed. In the days of Jael, so the author of Deborah's Song tells us, circuitous side-tracks were the only accessible routes. In the un-settled condition of Israel those who journeyed were forced to seek their goal by roundabout ways.

But, at other times, though the open road is clear, and there is no obstacle on the way of com-mon trade, the traveller may of choice turn to the by-ways and hedges. Not that he hates the wider track, but he may also love the less frequented, narrower paths, which carry him into nooks and glades, whence, after shorter or longer detours, he reaches the highway again. Not only has he been refreshed, but he has won, by forsaking the main road, a fuller appreciation of its worth.

Originally written in 1913 for serial publication, the papers collected in this volume were designed with some unity of plan. Branching off the main line of Hebraic development, there are many by-paths of the kind referred to above—by-paths lead-ing to pleasant places, where it is a delight to linger

5

for a while. Some of the lesser expressions of the Jewish spirit disport themselves in those out-of-the-way places. Though oft neglected, they do not deserve to be treated as negligible.

None can surely guide another to these places. But the first qualification of a guide, a qualification which may atone for serious defects, is that he himself enjoys the adventure. In the present instance this qualification may be claimed. For the writer has turned his attention chiefly to his own favorites, choosing books or parts of books which appealed to him in a long course of reading, and which came back to him with fragrant memories as he set about reviewing some of the former intimates of his leisure hours. The review is not formal; the method is that of the causerie, not of the essay. Some of the books are of minor value, curiosities rather than masterpieces; in others the Jewish interest is but slight. Yet in all cases the object has been to avoid details, except in so far as details help even the superficial observer to get to the author's heart, to place him in the history of literature or culture. Not quite all the authors noted in this volume were Jews—the past tense is used because it was felt best to include no writers living when the volume was compiled. It seemed, however, right that certain types of non-Jewish workers in the Hebraic field ought to find a place, partly from a sense of gratitude, partly because, without laboring the point, the writer conceives that as all cultures have many points in common, so it is well to bear in mind that many cultures have contributed their share to produce that complex entity—the Jewish spirit. Complex yet harmonious, influenced from without yet dominated by a strong inner and original power, the Jewish spirit reveals itself in these by-paths as clearly as on the main line.

But, though some such general idea runs through the volume, it was the author's intention to interest rather than instruct, to suggest the importance of certain authors and books, perhaps to rouse the reader to probe deeper than the writer himself has done into subjects of which here the mere surface is touched. The writer could have added indefinitely to these papers, but this selection is long enough to argue against extending it, at all events for the present.

Having decided to stray into the by-paths, it sometimes became necessary to resist the temptation to turn to the main road. This necessity accounts for another fact. Fewer books are treated

of the older period. For the older period is dominated by Bible and Talmud, and these were
ex hypothesi outside the range. So, too, the scholastic masterpieces and the greater products of
mysticism and law are passed over. Yet, though
the writer did not consciously start with such a design, it will be seen that accidentally a great fact
or two betray themselves. One is that, in the Jewish variety, technical learning can never be wholly
dissociated from what we more commonly name
literature. Some books which, at first sight, are
merely the expression of scholarly specialism are
seen, on investigation, to belong to culture in the
æsthetic no less than in the rational or legal sense.
Again, there becomes apparent the vital truth that
Jewish thought, dependent as it always has been
on environment, is also independent. For we see
how Jews in the midst of Hellenistic absolutism remained pragmatical, how under the medieval devotion to a stock-taking of the past Jews were to a
certain extent creative, and how the modernist tendency to disintegration was resisted by an impulse
towards constructiveness.

But, to repeat what has already been indicated,
the author had no such grave intentions as these.
Many of the papers appeared in a popular weekly,

the London *Jewish World,* the editor of which kindly conceded to the writer the privilege of collecting them into a book. Some, however, were specially written for this volume. All have been considerably revised, in the effort to make them more worthy of the reader's attention. The writer feels that this effort, despite the valuable help rendered by Dr. Halper while the proofs were under correction, has been imperfectly successful. The papers can have little in them to deserve attention. Nevertheless there is this to be urged. Some of the topics raised are apt to be ignored. Yet it is not only from the outstanding masterpieces of literature that we may learn wisdom and derive pleasure. " A small talent," said Joubert, " if it keeps within its limits and rightly fulfils its task, may reach the goal just as well as a greater one." This remark may be applied to what may seem to many the minor products of genius or talent. Hence, be they termed minor or major, the books discussed in this volume were worthy of consideration. Beyond doubt most of them belong to the category of the significant and some of them even attain the rank of the epoch-making. And so, without further preface, these papers are offered to those familiar as well as to those unfamiliar with the works themselves. For to both classes may be applied the Latin poet's invocation: " Now learn ye to love that loved never; and ye that have loved, love anew."

CONTENTS

CONTENTS

CONTENTS

ILLUSTRATIONS

PART I

Part I

THE STORY OF AHIKAR

We are happily passing out of the critical obsession, under which it was a sign of ignorance to attribute a venerable age to the records of the past. All the old books were written yesterday, or at earliest the day before! Facts, however, are stubborn; and facts, as they come to light, justify and re-affirm our fathers' faith in the antiquity of the world's literature. The story of Ahikar is a good illustration.

In the course of the Book of Tobit more than once *Achiachar* or *Ahikar* is mentioned. These allusions are verbal only, but in one scene the reference is more precise. The pious Tobit on his death-bed bids his son " consider what Nadab (Nadan) did to Achiachar, who brought him up " (14. 10).

What did Nadan do, and who was Ahikar? It is only within recent years that a complete answer has become possible to these questions. The older commentators on the Apocrypha were much worried by the allusion, and had to be content with the blindest guesses. Some versions of Tobit had, in place of the words quoted above, the following: " Consider how Aman treated Achiachar, who brought him up." Hence the suggestion arose that the reference was to Haman and Mordecai. But the Book of Esther does not hint that Mordecai had " brought up " Haman, and was then repaid by the latter's ingratitude.

But in 1880, G. Hoffmann discovered the clue. He recognized that Tobit's references were paralleled in a story found in Aesop's Fables and in the Arabian Nights, but much more fully recorded in the Story of Ahikar preserved in several versions, such as Syriac, Arabic, and Armenian. The story, briefly told in those fuller records, is as follows:

The hero is Ahikar. The name probably means something like *My Brother is Precious,* or *A Brother of Preciousness,* or possibly (as Dr. Halper suggests) *A Man of Honor.* He was grand vizier of Sennacherib, the king of Assyria. Noted for wisdom as for statesmanship, he rose to a position of the highest dignity and wealth. But he had no son. He, accordingly, adopted his infant nephew Nadan, and reared him with loving care. He furnished him with eight nurses, fed him on honey, clothed him in fine linen and silk, and

18

made him lie on choice carpets. The boy grew
big, and shot up like a cedar; whereupon Ahikar
started to teach him book-lore and wisdom. Nadan was introduced to the king, who readily
agreed to regard the youth as his minister's son, and
made promise of future favors to one in whom his
faithful vizier was so much interested. The narrative then breaks off to give in detail the wise maxims
which Ahikar sought to instil into Nadan; maxims
which have parallels in many literatures, including
the rabbinic. Now, Ahikar was grievously mistaken in the character of his nephew. Nadan
seemed to listen to his uncle's wisdom, but all the
while considered his monitor a dotard and a bore.
The young man began to reveal his true disposition; his cruelties to man and beast were such that
Ahikar protested, and offended Nadan by preferring a brother of the latter. Nadan, in revenge,
plotted Ahikar's downfall. By means of forged
letters, the old vizier was condemned for treachery,
though the executioner, mindful of a similar act of
mercy previously shown to himself, secretly spared
Ahikar's life. Nor was the day distant when Sennacherib bewailed the loss of Ahikar's services.
Menacing messages came from Egypt of a kind
which it needed an Ahikar to deal with. To the

19

king's joy, Ahikar was brought out from his hiding-place; he was again taken to court, and despatched to Egypt.

Here, once more, the narrative is interrupted to tell the details of these Egyptian experiences; how Ahikar satisfied the Pharaoh's plan of " raising a castle betwixt heaven and earth " by placing boys on the backs of eaglets, and how he countered the puzzling questions of the Egyptian sages. Thus, bidden to weave a rope out of sand, he bored five holes in the eastern wall of the palace, and when the sun entered the holes he sprinkled sand in them, and " the sun's furrow (path) began to appear as if the sand were twined in the holes." Then, again, the king of Egypt ordered that a broken upper millstone should be brought in. " Ahikar," said the king, " sew up for us this broken mill-stone." Ahikar, who throughout tells his story in the first person, was not daunted. " I went and brought a nether millstone, and cast it down before the king, and said to him: My lord the king, since I am a stranger here, and have not the tools of my craft with me, bid the cobblers cut me strips from this lower millstone which is the fellow of the upper millstone; and forthwith I will sew it together." The king laughed. Ahikar scored all round, and returned home to Assyria laden with the revenues of Egypt.

The third part of the story relates how Nadan was given over to Ahikar. His uncle bound him with iron chains, and " struck him a thousand blows on the shoulders and a thousand and one on his loins "; and while Nadan was thus imprisoned in the porch of the palace door, living on " bread by weight and water by measure," being compelled willy-nilly to listen, Ahikar proceeded with further lessons in wisdom. " My son," he says, " he who does not hear with his ears, they make him to hear with the scruff of his neck." Then there follow many wonderful parables, which (as with the maxims) are similar to those in many literatures. " Thereat," ends the tale, " Nadan swelled up like a bag, and died. And to him that doeth good, what is good shall be recompensed; and to him that doeth evil, what is evil shall be rewarded. But he that diggeth a pit for his neighbor, filleth it with his own stature. And to God be glory, and His mercy be upon us. Amen."

What was the original of this story? Nothing in the romance of its incidents, or in the marvel of the spread of it and its maxims and its incorporated fables throughout the folk-lore of humanity, ex-

ceeds the dramatic fact that a large fragment of
the tale, in Aramaic, has been found in Egypt
among other Jewish papyri of the fifth century before the Christian era! The discovery proves many
things, among them two being most significant.
First, the Ahikar story is far older than people
used to think, and thus the theory that the story of
Ahikar was invented to *explain* the reference in
Tobit is once for all disproved. Second, it is at
least tenable that the original language was Aramaic and the story Jewish. Here, at all events, we
have unquestionable evidence that there must have
been among the Jews, nearly 2,400 years ago, an
impulse towards that species of popular tale which
so deeply affected the literature and poetry of the
world. Ahikar, it has even been suggested, is the
ultimate source of at least one of the New Testament parables. But, more generally, now that we
know that the story of Ahikar was at so early a
date current among Jews, we shall be more plausibly able to justify the belief, long ago held by some,
that Aesop and other similar collections of fables
do truly come from Jewish originals. At any rate,
ancient Jewish parallels must have been in circu-
lation.

So much for the main results of the discovery. Small details of interest abound. Tobit bade his son: "Pour out thy bread and thy wine on the graves of the righteous (4. 17)." All sorts of changes have been suggested in the text. But the saying is found in the versions of Ahikar, and may be accepted as genuine. It is not necessarily a pagan rite; it has analogy with the funeral meal which long prevailed (and still prevails) as a Jewish custom. Even more interesting seems another detail (of the Syriac Version), which the writers on the books of Ahikar and Tobit have overlooked. When Tobit's son starts on his quest, his dog goes with him. This is a remarkable touch. Nowhere else in ancient Jewish literature does the dog appear as man's companion. Nowhere else? Yes, in one other place—in the story of Ahikar. "My son," says the vizier to Nadan, "strike with stones the dog that has left his own master and followed after thee." Here we see the dog regarded as a comrade, to be forcibly discouraged if he show signs of infidelity. There must have been a period, therefore, when the olden Jews considered the dog in a light quite other than that which afterwards became usual.

PHILO ON THE "CONTEMPLATIVE LIFE"

Much depends on the mood of the hour. Maimonides, in his *Eight Chapters* and in the opening section of his *Code,* acutely remarks that though excess in any moral direction is vicious, nevertheless it may be necessary for a man to practise an extreme in order to bring himself back from the other extreme into the middle path of virtue. Or, to use another phrase of the same philosopher, it is with the soul as with the body. To adjust the equilibrium it is proper to apply force on the side opposite to that which is over-balanced.

Hence it is not surprising to find Philo speaking, as it were, with two voices on the subject of the ascetic life. In the Alexandria of his day there was at one time prevalent a cult of self-renunciation. This cult had special attraction for the young and fashionable. They joined ascetic societies, and, in the name of religion, abandoned all participation in worldly affairs. Philo denounced these boyish millionaire recluses in fine style.

Wealth was not to be abused, true; it was, however, to be used. " Shun not the world, but live well in it," he cried. Do not avoid the festive board, but behave like gentlemen over your wine. It is all beautifully said, though I have modernized Philo's terms somewhat. " Be drunk with sobriety " is, however, one of Philo's very own phrases.

But there is this other side to consider. Alexandria was the very hotbed of luxury and extravagance. People speak about the inequalities of modern civilization, and seem to imagine that it is a new thing for a slum and a palace to exist side by side. But this was exactly the condition in Alexandria at about the beginning of the Christian era. Its busy and gorgeous bazaars, as Mr. F. C. Conybeare has said, blazed with products and wares imported and designed to tickle the palates and adorn the persons of the aristocracy. The same marts had another aspect, narrow and noisy, foul with misery and disease. Wealth and vice rubbed shoulders. Passing through such scenes, Philo might well be driven to see the superiority of asceticism over indulgence. Religion after all is renunciation. Idolatry, said Philo, dwarfs a man's soul, Judaism enlarges it. Idolatry may be compatible with " strong wine and dainty dishes," Judaism prefers a meal of bread and hyssop. In speaking thus, Philo reminds us of the Pharisaic saying: "A morsel with salt shalt thou eat, and water drink by measure, thou shalt sleep upon the ground, and live a life of painfulness, the while thou toilest in the Torah" (Pirke Abot 6. 4.). The association of "plain living" with "high thinking" could not be more emphatically expressed.

Few scholars nowadays doubt the Philonean authorship of the treatise "On the Contemplative Life." Conybeare, Cohn and Wendland have convinced us all, or nearly all, that the work is really Philo's. At first sight, no doubt, it was easier to suppose that the book was not his. It seems too cordial in its praise of seclusion, and comes too near the monastic spirit. But the Essenes were Jewish enough, and Philo's Therapeutae are essentially like the Essenes. "Therapeutae" is a Greek word which literally means "Servants," and was used to denote "Worshippers of God." The community of Therapeutae, according to Philo's description, was settled upon a low hill overlooking Lake Mareotis, not far from Alexandria. We need not go into details. These people adopted a severely simple life, each dwelling alone, spending the day in his private "holy room," passing the hours

without food, but occupied with the Law, the
Prophets, and the Psalms. On the Sabbath, however, they abandoned their isolation, and met in
common assembly, to listen to discourses. The
"common sanctuary" was a double enclosure,
divided by a wall of three or four cubits, so as to
separate the women from the men. Women
formed part of the audience, " having the same zeal
and following the same mode of life," all practising
celibacy. Men and women alike, or at least the
most zealous of them, well-nigh fasted throughout
the week, " having accustomed themselves, as they
say the grasshoppers do, to live upon air; for the
song of these, I suppose, assuages the feeling of
want." Their Sabbath meal was held in common,
for they regarded " the seventh day as in a manner
all holy and festal," and, therefore, " deem it worthy of peculiar dignity." The diet, however, " com-
prises nothing expensive, but only cheap bread; and
its relish is salt, which the dainty among them prepare with hyssop; and for drink they have water
from the spring." For, continues Philo, " they
propitiate the mistresses Hunger and Thirst, which
nature has set over mortal creatures, offering nothing that can flatter them, but merely such useful
food as life cannot be supported without. For this

27

reason they eat only so as not to be hungry, and drink only so as not to thirst, avoiding all surfeit as dangerous and inimical to body and soul." There is only one relaxation of this severity. No wine is brought to table, but such of the more aged as are " of a delicate habit of life " are permitted to drink their water hot.

Of course, the main tendency of Judaism has been in another direction. Fascinating though Philo's picture of the community of Therapeutae is, yet it cannot be felt to be a model for ordinary men and women. From time to time, indeed, Jews (like the disciples of Isaac Luria) followed much the same course of life. But most have been unwilling or unable to accept such an ideal as worthy of imitation. It is not at all certain that Philo meant it to be a model; anyhow, as we have seen, he was not always in the same mood. Judah ha-Levi opens the third part of his *Khazari* with just this distinction between the ideal circumstances, under which the ascetic life may be admirable, and the normal conditions, under which it is culpable. " When the Divine Presence was still in the Holy Land among the people capable of prophecy, some few persons lived an ascetic life in deserts " with good results. But nowadays, continues Judah ha-Levi, " he who in our time and place and people, ' whilst no open vision exists ' (I Samuel 3. 1), the desire for study being small, and persons with a natural talent for it absent, would like to retire into ascetic solitude, only courts distress and sickness for soul and body." The real pietist, he concludes, is not the man who ignores his senses, but the man who rules over them. And this was really the view of Philo also, as we find it in his other works. " The bad man," he says, " treats pleasure as the *summum bonum,* the good man as a necessity, for without pleasure nothing happens among mortals." And so he counsels men to follow the avocations of ordinary life, and not to disdain ambition. " In fine, it is necessary that they who would concern themselves with things divine should, first of all, have discharged the duties of man. It is a great folly to think we can reach a comprehension of the greater when we are unable to overcome the less. Be first known by your excellence in things human, in order that you may apply yourselves to excellence in things divine." (I take these quotations from C. G. Montefiore's brilliant *Florilegium Philonis,* which he ought to reprint.) Philo undoubtedly thought more highly of the contemplative than of the practical life. But in this last

29

passage he gets very near the truth when he treats the former as only noble when it is based on the latter. It is another aspect of the rabbinic truth that " not study but conduct " is the end of virtue. Philo does not contradict this truth; he offers to our inspection the reverse side of the same shield.

One other point remains. The reader of Philo's eulogy of the Contemplative Life must be struck by the gaiety of these ascetics. Again and again Philo speaks of their joyousness. They " compose songs and hymns to God in divers strains and measures." There is nothing morose about them. They build up the edifice of virtue on a foundation of continence, but it is a cheerful devotion after all. Above all is the music, the singing. They have " many melodies " to which they sing old songs or newly written poems. One sings in solo, and then they all " give out their voices in unison, all the men and all the women together " joining in " the catches and refrains," and " a full and harmonious symphony results." Philo grows ecstatic. " Noble are the thoughts, and noble the words of their hymn, yea, and noble the choristers. But the end and aim of thought and words and choristers alike is holiness." And this summary ought to be applicable to every form of Jewish life, to those phases particularly which reject the excesses of asceticism. "Serve the Lord with joy," says the hundredth Psalm. True we must have the joy; but we must also not omit the service.

JOSEPHUS AGAINST APION

" Buffon, the great French naturalist," as Matthew Arnold reminds us, " imposed on himself the rule of steadily abstaining from all answer to attacks made upon him." This attitude of dignified silence has often been commended. In one of his wisest counsels, Epictetus recommended his friends not to defend themselves when attacked. If a man speaks ill of you, said the Stoic, you should only reply: " Good sir, you must be ignorant of many others of my faults, or you would not have mentioned only these." An older than Epictetus gave similar advice. Sennacherib's emissary, the Rabshakeh, had insolently assailed Hezekiah; " but the people held their peace, for the king's commandment was: Answer him not " (II Kings 18. 36). On this last text a fine homily may be found in a printed volume of the late Simeon Singer's Sermons. Mr. Singer illustrated his counsel of restraint by a reference to Josephus. Apion more than 1,800 years ago had traduced the Jews, and Josephus demolished his slanders in " as powerful a piece of controversial literature as is to be found." " But," continued the preacher, " note the irony of the situation. But for Josephus' reply, Apion would long have been forgotten "; not his name, but certainly the details of his typical anti-Semitism.

This fact, however, does not carry with it the conclusion that Josephus rendered his people an ill-service. There are two orders of Apologetics— the destructive and the constructive. *Apologia* was originally a legal term which denoted the speech of the defendant against the plaintiff's charges. As we know abundantly well from the forensic giants of the classical oratory—such as Demosthenes and Cicero—these defences were largely made up of abuse of the other side. Josephus was an apt pupil of these masters. His abuse of Apion leaves nothing to the imagination; everything is formulated, and with scathing particularity. Josephus, it is true, does not seem to have been unjust. Rarely, if ever, has an out-and-out anti-Semite possessed a pleasing personality. Apion was a grammarian of note, but there is much evidence as to his unamiable characteristics. The emperor Tiberius, who knew a braggart when he saw one, called Apion " cymbalum mundi "—a world-drum, making the universe ring with his ostentatious garrulity. Aulus Gellius records his vanity; Pliny accuses him of falsehood and charlatanism. Josephus was, therefore, not going beyond the facts when he describes him as a scurrilous mountebank. It cannot be denied, moreover, that Josephus scores heavily against his opponent, in solid argument as well as in verbal invective. If the Jewish historian made Apion immortal, it was a deathless infamy that he secured for him.

Certainly, too, Josephus successfully rebuts Apion's specific libels: the most silly of them, however, antedated Apion and survived him. Tacitus, indeed, seems to have gathered his own weapons out of Apion's armory, and the Roman repeats the Alexandrian's libel that in Jerusalem an ass was adored. Those who are interested in this legend of ass-worship may turn to a learned article by Dr. S. Krauss in the *Jewish Encyclopedia* (vol. ii, p. 222). It has been suggested that the charge arose from a confusion between the Jews and certain Egyptian or Dionysian sects. Others believe that at bottom there lies a misunderstanding of the " foundation-stone," which, according to talmudic tradition, was placed in the ark during the second temple. The upper millstone was called by the Greeks " the ass," for its tedious turning resembled an ass's burdensome activity. But, be the explanation what it may, the ignorance of a professed expert such as Apion was inexcusable. Yet, most grimly amusing of all Apion's charges is his repetition of the ever-recurrent libel that the Jews were haters of their fellow-men. Never was there a more perfect illustration of Aesop's fable of the wolf and the lamb: the hated transformed into the haters! Apion was a fine type of lover. Off to Rome went he, leading the Alexandrian deputation against the Jews (who were championed by Philo), denouncing them to the Cæsar, and using every artifice to incite the imperial animosity. With a heart bitter with hostility, Apion would be a fitting assailant of the " haters of mankind." It is one of the curiosities of fate that, apart from what Josephus has told of him, Apion is best remembered as the author or transmitter of the story of Androcles and the lion. Apion was neither the first nor the last to have a kindlier feeling for a wild beast than for a fellow-man.

To all the points adduced by Apion Josephus makes a triumphant answer. But his book, termed rather inaptly *Against Apion,* would not deserve its repute merely because it demolished a particularly malignant opponent. The book really belongs to Apologetic of the second of the two orders distinguished above. Higher far than the destructive Apologetic is the constructive, which rebuts a falsehood, not by denouncing the liar, but by presenting the truth. " Great is truth, and it will prevail," is the maxim of an ancient Jewish book (I Esdras 4. 41), a maxim well known in substance to Josephus himself (*Antiquities,* xi. 3). " Who ever knew truth put to the worse in a free and open encounter? " asks Milton. If we once give up confidence in the unconquerable power of truth to win in the end, we have already made an end of human hope. Apologetic, then, of the better type attaches itself to this belief in the inherent virtue of truth. It meets the enemy not with weapons similar to his own, but with a shield impervious to all weapons.

Josephus can sustain this test. Judged by the constructive standard, the treatise *Against Apion* is a masterpiece. That the Jews were an ancient people with an age-long record of honor, and not a race of recent and disreputable upstarts, Josephus proves by citations from older writers who, but for these citations, would be even less known than they now are. It is not, however, on such arguments that Josephus chiefly rests his case. The external history of the Jews, their glorious participation in the world's affairs—these are much.

But there is somthing which is far more. " As for ourselves, we neither inhabit a maritime country, *nor delight in commerce,* nor in such intercourse with other men as arises from it; but the cities we dwell in are remote from the sea, and as we have a fruitful country to dwell in, we take pains in cultivating it. *But our principal care of all is to educate our children well,* and to observe the laws, and we think it to be the most necessary business of our whole life to keep that religion that has been handed down to us " (i. 12). This passage is famous both for its denial of the supposed natural bent of Jews to commerce and for its assertion that education is the principal purpose of Jewish endeavor. Josephus, especially in the second book of his Apology, expounds Judaism as life and creed in glowing terms. This exposition is one of our main sources of information for the Judaism of the first century of the Christian era. His picture of life under the Jewish law is a panegyric, but praise is not always partiality. Is it an exaggerated claim that Josephus makes on behalf of Judaism? Surely not. " I make bold to say," exclaims Josephus in his peroration, " that we are become the teachers of other men in the greatest number of things, and those the most excellent. For what is more excellent

than unshakable piety? What is more just than obedience to the laws? And what is more advantageous
than mutual love and concord, and neither to be
divided by calamities, nor to become injurious and
seditious in prosperity, but to despise death when
we are in war, and to apply ourselves in peace to
arts and agriculture, while we are persuaded that
God surveys and directs everything everywhere.
If these precepts had either been written before by
others, or more exactly observed, we should have
owed them thanks as their disciples, but if it is plain
that we have made more use of them than other
men, and if we have proved that the original invention of them is our own, let the Apions and Molos,
and all others who delight in lies and abuse, stand
confuted."

There were grounds on which contemporary
Jews had just cause for complaint against Josephus.
He lacked patriotism. But only in the political
sense. When Judea was invaded, he did not stand
firm in resistance to Rome. But when Judaism was
calumniated, he was a true patriot. He stands high
in the honorable list of those who championed the
Jewish cause without thought of self. Or, rather,
such self-consciousness as he displays is communal,
not personal. When he pleads his people's cause,
his pettinesses vanish, he is every inch a Jew.

CAECILIUS ON THE SUBLIME

Favorable remarks on Hebrew literature are very rare in the Greek writers. One of the most significant is contained in the ninth section of Longinus' famous treatise on the Sublime.

This Greek author—it will soon be seen why the name Caecilius and not Longinus appears in the title of this article—analyses sublimity of style into five sources: 1) grandeur of thought; 2) spirited treatment of the passions; 3) figures of thought and speech; 4) dignified expression; 5) majesty of structure. Longinus points out that the first two conditions of sublimity depend mainly on natural endowments, whereas the last three derive assistance from art.

It is when illustrating the first of the five elements that our author refers to the Bible. The most important of all conditions of the Sublime is "a certain lofty cast of mind." Such sublimity is "the image of greatness of soul." As he beautifully says: "It is only natural that their words should be full of sublimity, whose thoughts are full of majesty." Longinus, accordingly, refuses to

praise without reserve Homer's picture of the
" Battle of the Gods ":

> A trumpet sound
> Rang through the air, and shook the Olympian height,
> Then terror seized the monarch of the dead,
> And, springing from his throne, he cried aloud
> With fearful voice, lest the earth, rent asunder
> By Neptune's mighty arm, forthwith reveal
> To mortal and immortal eyes those halls
> So drear and dank, which e'en the gods abhor.

An impious medley, Longinus terms this, a perfect hurly-burly, terrible in its forcefulness, but
overstepping the bounds of decency. (I take these
and other phrases from Mr. H. L. Havell's fine
translation). Far to be preferred are those
Homeric passages which " exhibit the divine nature
in its true light as something spotless, great, and
pure." He instances the lines in the Iliad on
Poseidon, though there does not seem much to
choose between them and the passage condemned
above. But then follows the remarkable paragraph which is the reason why I have chosen
Longinus for a place in this gallery: " And thus
also the lawgiver of the Jews, no ordinary man,
having formed an adequate conception of the
Supreme Being, gave it adequate expression in the

40

opening words of his Laws: *God said: Let there be light, and there was light; let there be earth, and there was earth.*"

Few will dispute that this passage in Genesis belongs to the sublimest order of literature. It is of the utmost interest that Longinus (whoever he was) should have recognized this fact. Whoever he was—whether the true Longinus, or an unknown rhetorician of the first century. Whether it belongs to the age of Augustus or Aurelian, it is equally noteworthy that the Greek writer should have admitted that the sublime might be exhibited by Moses as well as by Homer. It is quite clear, however, that Longinus did not take his quotation from the Hebrew Bible itself or from the Greek translation. Had he known the Bible, he must have made much fuller use of it. Read his analysis of the sublime quoted above. He could, and would, have illustrated every one of his five conditions from the Bible, had he been acquainted with it. Moreover, the quotation from Genesis is inexact. There is no text: *God said: Let there be earth, and there was earth.* Obviously, as Théodore Reinach points out, the reference is taken from the sense, not the words, of Genesis i. 9 and 10. Longinus, therefore, either knew it from hearsay, or he had found the quotation in the course of his reading.

This latter suggestion was made as long ago as 1711 by Schurzfleisch—how Matthew Arnold would have jibed at a man with such a name commenting on the *Sublime!* Longinus quotes a previous treatise on the Sublime by a certain Caecilius. His predecessor, says Longinus, wasted his efforts " in a thousand illustrations of the nature of the Sublime," while he failed to define the subject. Be that as it may, Longinus quotes Caecilius several times, especially for these very illustrations. It is by no means improbable, then, that Longinus' reference to Genesis was derived from Caecilius, who may have paraphrased from memory rather than have quoted with the Bible before him. Now, Suidas informs us that Caecilius was reported to be a Jew. Reinach (*Revue des Études Juives,* vol. xxvi, pp. 36-46) has provided full ground for accepting the information of Suidas, which is now generally adopted as true.

Caecilius belonged to the first century of the current era, and, born in Sicily, the offspring of a slave, he betook himself as a freedman to Rome, where he won considerable note as a writer on rhetoric. *The Characters of the Ten Orators* was one of his most important books; several histories are ascribed to him; and, as we have seen, he wrote a formal treatise on the Sublime, which gave rise to the better-known work attributed to Longinus. It is not clear whether Caecilius was a born Jew or a proselyte. Probably the theory that best fits the facts is that of Schürer. We may suppose that the rhetorician's father was brought to Rome as a Jewish slave by Pompey, and was then sold to a Sicilian. In Sicily, the son, who bore the name Archagathos, received a Greek education, and was freed by a Roman of the Caecilius clan. The freedman would drop his own name, and adopt the family name of his benefactor, according to common practice. Schürer offers a very acute, and I think conclusive, argument against the view that Caecilius was a convert to Judaism. A proselyte would have exhibited much more zeal for his new faith. In the works of Caecilius, I may add, his Judaism seems more a reminiscence than a vital factor. It is, on the whole, more likely that he came of Jewish ancestry than that he was himself a new-made Jew. Reinach contends that *because* he was a proselyte, Caecilius knew the Bible only superficially, and hence arose his misquotation of Genesis. Is that a probable view to take? If we

43

conceive, with Schürer, that the father of Caecilius, a born Jew, had passed through such vicissitudes, being carried a slave from Syria to Rome, transferred into an alien environment in Sicily, we can well understand that the son would possess but a superficial memory of the Bible. On the other hand, a proselyte would have become a devotee to the Scriptures, the beauties of which had burst upon his mind for the first time. He would not misquote. The chief Jewish translators of the Bible into Greek (apart, of course, from the oldest Alexandrian version) were, curiously enough, proselytes to Judaism. Perhaps it would be too far-fetched to suggest that Caecilius had a particular reason to remember the first chapter of Genesis. His original name, Archagathos, is not a bad translation of the Hebrew " very good " (*tob meod*) which occurs prominently in the story of the Creation.

Unfortunately, none of the works of Caecilius is preserved. We know him only by a few fragments. Plutarch described him as " eminent in all things," yet neither Schürer in his earlier editions, nor Graetz in any edition, placed him where he ought to be—to use Reinach's phraseology—in the phalanx of the great Jewish Hellenists, with Aristobulus, Philo, and Josephus. Caecilius was the

44

restorer of Atticism in literature, a piquant rôle for a Jew to play. Yet it is a part the Jew has often filled. An instructive essay could be written on the services rendered by Hebrews to the spread of Hellenism, not merely in the ancient world, but also in the medieval and modern civilizations.

THE PHOENIX OF EZEKIELOS

" The plumage," writes Herodotus (ii. 73), " is partly red, partly golden, while the general form and size are almost exactly like the eagle." The Greek historian was describing the phoenix, the fabled bird which lived for five hundred years. According to another version, she then consumed herself in fire, and from the ashes emerged again in youthful freshness. Herodotus likens the phoenix to the eagle, and the reader of some of the Jewish commentaries on the last verse of Isaiah 40 and the fifth verse of Psalm 103 will find references to similar ideas. In particular to be noted is Kimhi's citation of Sa'adya's reference to the belief that the eagle acquired new wings every twelve years, and lived a full century. Such fancies easily attached themselves to Isaiah's phrase and to the psalmist's words: " Thy youth is renewed like the eagle." The biblical metaphors, in sober fact, merely allude to the fullness of life, high flight, and vigor of the eagle; there is nothing whatever that is mythical about them.

What passes for one of the most famous descriptions of the phoenix is contained in the well-known Greek drama of the Exodus (or rather *Exagogê*) written by the Jewish poet, Ezekielos. This writer probably flourished rather more than a century before the Christian era. It is commonly supposed that he lived in the capital of the Ptolemies, in Alexandria; but it has been suggested by Kuiper that his home was not in Egypt, but in Palestine, in Samaria. If that be so, it is a remarkable phenomenon. We should not wonder that a Jew in *Alexandria* composed Greek dramas on biblical themes, with the twofold object of presenting the history of Israel in attractive form and of providing a substitute for the heathen plays which monopolized the ancient theatre. But that such dramas should be produced soon after the Maccabean age in *Palestine* would imply an unexpected continuity of the influences of Greek manners in the homeland of the Jews. Ere we could accept the theory of a Palestinian origin for Ezekielos, we should need far stronger arguments than Kuiper adduces (*Revue des Études Juives,* vol. xlvi, p. 48, *seq.*).

The drama of the *Exodus*—which was apparently written to be performed—follows the biblical

story with some closeness. We are now, however,
interested in a single episode, preserved for us
among the fragments of Ezekielos as quoted by
Eusebius (*Prep. Evangel,* ix. 30). A beautiful
picture of the twelve springs of Elim and of its
seventy palms is followed by a description of the
extraordinary bird that appeared there. I take
the passage from Gifford's *Eusebius* (iii, p. 475).
A character of the play, after the Greek manner, is
reporting to Moses:

> Another living thing we saw, more strange
> And marvellous than man e'er saw before,
> The noblest eagle scarce was half as large;
> His outspread wings with varying colors shone;
> The breast was bright with purple, and the legs
> With crimson glowed, and on the shapely neck
> The golden plumage shone in graceful curves;
> The head was like a gentle nestling's formed;
> Bright shone the yellow circlet of the eye
> On all around, and wondrous sweet the voice.
> The king he seemed of all the winged tribe,
> As soon was proved; for birds of every kind
> Hovered in fear behind his stately form;
> While like a bull, proud leader of the herd,
> Foremost he marched with swift and haughty step.

Gifford has no hesitation in accepting the common identification of this bird with the phoenix.
Obviously, however, Ezekielos says nothing of the

48

mythical properties of the bird; he merely presents to us a super-eagle of gorgeous plumage and splendid stature, unnatural but not supernatural. Even the magnificence of the superb bird pictured by Ezekielos is less bizarre than we find it in other authors. Ezekielos' figures sink into insignificance beside those of Lactantius, who tells us that the bird's monstrous eyes resembled twin hyacinths, from the midst of which flashed and quivered a bright flame. If Ezekielos really refers to the phoenix, how does it come into the drama at all? Gifford has this note: " There is no mention in Exodus of the phoenix or any such bird, but the twelve palm-trees (*phoenix*) at Elim may have suggested the story of the phoenix to the poet, just as in the poem of Lactantius. *Phoenix* 70, the tree is said to have been named from the bird." The word *phoenix* has, I may add, a romantic history. It means, literally, *Phoenician*. Now, certain of the Phoenician race were the reputed discoverers and first users of purple-red or crimson dyes. Hence these colors were named after them, *Phoenix* or *Phoenician*. The Greek translation, in Isaiah 1. 18, renders " scarlet " by *Phoenician*. The epithet was applied equally to red cattle, to the bay horse, to the *date-palm* and its fruit. It was also used of the fabulous bird because of its colorings. Gifford supposes, then, that Ezekielos knowing of the *palms* reached at Elim in the early wanderings of Israel, introduced the *bird* into his drama. The palms at Elim are indeed described by this very word (Phoenician) in the Greek translation of the Bible which Ezekielos used (Exodus 15. 27). The *lulab* is also termed *phoenix* in the Greek of Leviticus 23. 40.

The explanation seems at first sight as plausible as it is clever. But it involves a serious difficulty. For Ezekielos in a previous passage has already described the Phoenician palm-trees at considerable length. The passage has been partly noted above, but it is musical enough to be worth citing as a whole:

> See, my Lord Moses, what a spot is found,
> Fanned by sweet airs from yonder shady grove;
> For as thyself mayest see, there lies the stream,
> And thence at night the fiery pillar shed
> Its welcome guiding light. A meadow there
> Beside the stream in grateful shadow lies,
> And a deep glen in rich abundance pours
> From out a single rock twelve sparkling springs.
> There, tall and strong, and laden all with fruit,
> Stand palms threescore and ten; and plenteous grass,
> Well watered, gives sweet pasture to our flocks.

It seems incredible that the poet who thus describes the palms could then have proceeded to confuse the palms with a bird. Ezekielos does not use the epithet Phoenician in his account of the latter. Thus the theory breaks down. How then is the passage to be explained? As it seems to me, in another and simpler way.

" There is no mention in Exodus of the phoenix or any such bird," says Gifford. He is right as to the phoenix, but is he right as to " any such bird "? My readers will at once remember the forceful metaphor in the nineteenth chapter of Exodus: "And Moses went up unto God, and the Lord called unto him out of the mountain, saying: ' Thus shalt thou say to the house of Jacob, and tell the children of Israel: Ye have seen what I did unto the Egyptians, and how I bore you *on eagles' wings,* and brought you unto Myself.' " The Mekilta interprets the words to refer to the rapidity with which Israel was assembled for the departure from Egypt, and to the powerful protection which it afterwards enjoyed. But we may also find in the same words the clue to the poet's fancy. " I bore you on eagles' wings," says the Pentateuch. No doubt the phrases of Herodotus, as well as those of Hesiod, were familiar to Ezekielos. With these in mind, he introduced a super-eagle, figuratively mentioned in the book of Exodus, and gave to it substance and life. He personified the metaphor. It would be a perfectly legitimate exercise of poetical license. The description is bizarre. But it is not mythological, and it has little to do with the phoenix of fable.

THE LETTER OF SHERIRA

Though all Israelites are brothers, they do not admit that they are all members of the same family. " Of good genealogy " is the proudest boast of the modern, as it was of the talmudic, Jew. It is, accordingly, not wonderful that we find our notabilities from Hillel to Abarbanel claiming, or having assigned to them, descent from the Davidic line. Of Sherira the same was said. He ruled over the academy in Pumbeditha during the last third of the tenth century. A scion of the royal house of Judah, he was rightful heir to the exilarchy, yet preferred the socially lower, but academically higher, office of Gaon. The Gaon's sway was religious and scholastic; the exilarch's secular and political. Sherira's ancestry might have given him the latter post, but for the former it was intrinsic, personal worth which qualified him and his famous son Hai. Who shall deny that he made a worthy choice?

Sherira's fame rests less on his general activities as Gaon than on the Letter which he wrote about the year 980, in response to questions formulated by Jacob ben Nissim, of Kairuwan. One of these questions retains, and will ever retain, its fascination, although the answer has now no vital interest. Historically the Letter has other claims to continued study. To quote Dr. L. Ginzberg (*Geonica,* i, p. 169) : " The lasting value of his epistle for us lies in the information Rabbi Sherira gives about the post-Talmudic scholars. On this period he is practically the only source we have." Without Sherira, the course of the traditional development would be a blank for a long interval after the close of the Talmud. " But," continues Dr. Ginzberg, " we shall be doing Rabbi Sherira injustice if we thought of him merely as a chronologist." And this same competent scholar launches out into the following eulogy of the Gaon: " The theories which he unfolds . . . . regarding the origin of the *Mishnah* . . . . and many other points important in the history of the Talmud and its problems, stamp Rabbi Sherira as one of the most distinguished historians, in fact, it is not an exaggeration to say, the most distinguished historian of literature among the Jews, not only of antiquity, but also in the middle ages, and during a large part of modern times."

54

This must suffice for the general estimate of Sherira's work. What is of more striking interest is just the one question, the answer to which does not much matter. As Dr. Neubauer formulated the question put to Sherira, it ran thus: " Was the Mishnah transmitted *orally* to the doctors of the Mishnah, or was it *written down* by the compiler himself? " Judah the Prince, we know, compiled the Mishnah, but did he leave it in an oral or a documentary form? Was it memorized or set down in script? The answer does not much matter, as I have said, for sooner or later the Mishnah *was* written out, and it is not of great consequence whether it was later or sooner. And it is as well that Sherira's answer matters little, for we do not know for certain what Sherira's answer was! Most authorities nowadays believe that the Gaon pronounced in favor of the written compilation; but this was not always the case. For Sherira's Letter was current in two versions which recorded opposite opinions. In the French form the oral alternative was accepted, but the Spanish text adopted the written theory. Which was the genuine view of Sherira? There are many reasons for preferring the Spanish version. As Dr. Neubauer points out, " books, letters, and responsa coming from the

East, reached Spain and Italy before they came to France and Germany." Hence the Spanish text is more likely to be primitive; while, when the Letter was carried further, it might easily have been altered so as to fall in with the talmudic prohibition against putting the traditional laws into writing. It will, again, come as a surprise to some to note another argument used by Dr. Neubauer in favor of the Spanish text. " From the greater consistency of the Aramaic dialect in the Spanish text, a dialect which, as we know from the Responsa of the Geonim, they used in their writings, it may be concluded that this (the Spanish) composition is the genuine one." The Gaonate was able to maintain a pretty thorough Jewish spirit without insisting on the use of Hebrew as the only medium of salvation. Actually Dr. Neubauer saw in the more consistent Aramaic of the Spanish text an indication of its superior authenticity over what may be called the French text!

But all these points are secondary. The real interest lies in this whole conception of an *oral book*. Tradition necessarily must be largely oral; ideas, maxims, and even defined rules of conduct not only can be, they must be, transmitted by word of mouth. But is there any possibility that a whole, elaborate book, or rather series of six books, should be put together and then trusted to memory? A new turn to the discussion was given by Prof. Gilbert Murray's Harvard Lectures on " The Rise of the Greek Epic." To him the Iliad of Homer appears in the guise of a " traditional book." No doubt the Mishnah belongs to a period separated from Homer by well-nigh a millennium. But the phrase holds. A *book* can be the outcome of tradition, can be carried on by it, expanded and elaborated, just as much as an oral code or history or poem. When, then, we speak of a traditional book, it does not necessarily mean that the book was not written down. The written words become precious, and the fact that they are written does not of itself spell finality or stagnation. There never was any danger of such an evil result until the age of printing and stereotyping. Nor can we conceive of a traditional book as the work of one mind. Judah the Prince neither began nor ended the chain of tradition because he wrote the Mishnah. There had been Mishnahs before him, just as there were developments of law after him.

Yet, on the other hand, it is not incredible that Judah the Prince's traditional book remained an unwritten book. It is improbable, but not at all

57

impossible. A modern lawyer of the first rank must hold in his mind quite as many decisions and principles as are contained in the Mishnah. Macaulay could repeat by heart the whole of the *Paradise Lost* and much else. Many a Talmudist of the present day must remember vast masses of the traditional Halakah. Before the age of printing, before copies of books became common and easily accessible, scholars must have been compelled to trust to their memory for many things for which we can turn to our reference libraries. When Maimonides compiled his great Code, he must have done a good deal of it from memory. Not that men's memories are worse now than they were. But we are now able to spare ourselves. It is not a good thing to use the memory unnecessarily. It should be reserved for essentials. What we can always get from books we need not keep in mind. Besides, in olden times men remembered better not because they had better memories, but because they had less to remember.

On the whole, however, it is safer to conclude that Judah the Prince made a contribution to written literature, that he set down at a particular moment (about 200 C. E.) the traditional book which had been writing itself for many decades, partly by the minds of the Rabbis, partly by their pens. He started the book on a new career of humane activity. Sherira and the Geonim were what they were because Judah the Prince was what he was. This is the essential fact about tradition. The more we give of our best to our age, the more chance is there for all future ages to transmit of their best to posterity.

NATHAN OF ROME'S DICTIONARY

A dictionary may seem an intruder in this gallery. The present series of cursory studies clearly is not concerned with works of technical scholarship. But the dictionary by Nathan, son of Jehiel, earns inclusion for two reasons. First, because when one surveys the expressions of the Jewish spirit, it is impossible to draw a line between learning and literature. Secondly, quite apart from this intimate general connection between the scholar and the man of letters, the dictionary of Nathan belongs specially to the course of culture. Among the Christian Humanists who, at the period of the Reformation, promoted the enlightenment of Europe, were not lacking appreciators of the services rendered to enlightenment by Nathan's *Aruk* (to give it its Hebrew title).

Nathan (born about 1035 and died in 1106) was an itinerant vendor of linen wares in his youth. He belonged to the family Degli Mansi, an Italian rendering of the Hebrew *Anaw* or *Meek*. The latter is still a rare but familiar Jewish surname. Legend has it that the founder of the Degli Mansi house was one of the original settlers introduced into Rome by Titus. At all events, the family had a long record of literary fame. Like many another merchant-traveller of the Middle Ages, Nathan made use of his earlier wanderings (as he did of his later journeys), to sit at the feet of all the Gamaliels of his age. Many and various were his teachers. He abandoned business when he returned to Rome after his father's death. He tells us how he made the arrangements for the interment, and here straightway we perceive that his *Aruk* is no ordinary dictionary. For in the poem, which he appends as a kind of retrospective preface, he records how sternly he had ever disapproved of the expenses incurred at Jewish funerals in his time. Protests were vain, but example was more fruitful. In place of the double cerements in common use, he laid his father in his tomb with a single shroud. This, he records, became the model for others to imitate. Death was a frequent visitor in his abode. Of his four sons, none survived the eighth year, one not even his eighth day. Grief did not crush him. " I found sorrow and trouble, then I called on the name of the Lord," he quotes. He proceeded to erect a house of another kind. Not of flesh and blood, but vital with the spirit of

Judaism, his *Aruk* is a monument more lasting than ten children.

In what, then, does the importance of the dictionary consist? It is, of course, primarily, what Graetz terms it, " a key to the Talmud." No doubt there were earlier compilations of a similar nature, but Nathan's book was the most renowned of its own age, and became the basis of every subsequent lexicon to the Talmud. Gentile and Jew, from Buxtorf to Dalman and from Musafia to Jastrow, employed it as the ground-work of their own lexicographical research. Moreover, it was again and again edited and enlarged; but we are not dealing here with bibliographical details. Suffice it to mention the final edition by Alexander Kohut. Kohut began his *Aruch Completum* while a European Rabbi in 1878, and finished it in New York in 1892. It is remarkable that two of the best modern lexicons to the Talmud (Kohut's in Hebrew and Jastrow's in English) both emanate from America.

Besides its value for understanding the text of the Talmud, Nathan's *Aruk* has earned other claims to fame. Nathan's dictionary marks an epoch, says Vogelstein. Consider the situation. The centre of Jewish authority was leaving Babylon. The last of the great literary Geonim—or *Excellencies,* as the heads of the Babylonian schools were called—died in the year 1038. Europe was replacing Asia as the scene of Jewish life. Was the old tradition to die? At the very moment of the crisis, three men arose to prevent the chain snapping. They were almost contemporaries, and their works supplemented each other. There was the Frenchman Rashi—the commentator; the Spaniard al-Fasi—the codifier; and the Italian Nathan—the lexicographer. Between them they re-established in Europe the tradition of the Gaonate. The Babylonian schools might come and go; they might for a time enjoy hegemony, and then fall into decay; but the Torah must go on forever!

The manner in which this dictionary carried on the tradition is easily told. Much of the lore it contains, explanations of words and of things, must have been *orally* acquired in direct conversations with those who were personally linked with the older *régime.* It is again full of quotations of the decisions and customary lore of the Babylonian schools. If on this side the *Aruk* has almost played out its part for us, it is not because those decisions and customs are less interesting to us than they were to our fathers. But we are now in possession of very

many of the gaonic writings in their original. We
have recovered several of the sources from which
Nathan drew. The Egyptian Genizah—that won-
derfully preserved mass of the relics of Hebrew
literature—has yielded its richest harvest just in
this field. We are getting to know more about the
thought and manner of life of the eighth to the
eleventh centuries than we know about our own
time. But for a long interval men's knowledge of
those centuries was largely derived from the *Aruk*.
As a source of information it is not even now super-
seded. There still remain authors whose names
and works would be lost but for Rabbi Nathan's
quotations.

Another aspect of the book which makes it so
valuable for the history of culture among the Jews
is the number of languages which Nathan uses.
What an array it is! Kohut enumerates (besides
Hebrew and Aramaic) Latin, Greek, Arabic,
Slavonic dialects, Persian, and Italian and allied
speeches. Nathan cannot have known all these
languages well. He certainly had little Latin and
less Greek, but he repeated what he had heard
from others or read in their books. It is remarkable, indeed, how well the sense of Greek words
was transmitted by Jewish writers who were igno-

rant of Greek. They often are not even aware that the words are Greek at all; they suggest the most impossible Semitic *derivations;* but they very rarely give the meanings incorrectly. This applies less to the Italian than to the German Jewish scholars. I mean that the former had, on the whole, a more intimate acquaintance with the classical idioms. In the case of Nathan's *Aruk* the languages cited do imply a wide and varied culture. Most interesting is Nathan's free use of Italian. Just as we learn from the glosses in Rashi's commentaries that the Jews of northern France spoke French, so we gather from Nathan's dictionary that the Jews of Rome must have used Italian as the medium of ordinary intercourse.

Nathan's *Aruk,* while, as we have seen, it was a link between the past and his present, was also part of the chain binding his present to the future. Nathan records the tradition as he received it, but he also points forward. Take one of his remarks, which is quoted by Güdemann. There is much in the Talmud on the subject of magic, and Nathan duly explains the terms employed. But he says: " All these statements about magic and amulets, I know neither their meaning nor their origin." Does the reader appreciate the extraordinary significance of the statement? Nathan, the bearer of tradition, yet sees that the newer order of things also has its claims. Tradition does not consist in the denial of science. And so, though a Gaon like Hai had a pretty considerable belief in demonology, Nathan cautiously expresses his scepticism. Even more emphatically, a little later, Ibn Ezra frankly asserted that he had no belief in demons. It may be questioned whether this enfranchisement from demonological conceptions could be matched in non-Jewish thought of so early a date. The *Aruk* assuredly points forwards as well as backwards.

And all this we derive from a dictionary! The *Aruk* obviously belongs to culture as well as to philology—if the two things really can be separated. The study of words is often the study of civilization. Max Müller maintained that if you could only tell the real history of words you would thereby be telling the real history of men. He carried the idea absurdly far; but Nathan's *Aruk* is a striking instance of at least the partial truth of the great Sanskrit scholar's contention.

THE SORROWS OF TATNU

Tatnu has a weird sound. But it is not the title of a fetich; it is not a personal name; it is not even a word at all. It is, indeed, a figure; but the figure it stands for is numerical. The letters which compose the Hebrew combination Tatnu amount to 856 (*taw* = 400; *taw* = 400; *nun* = 50; *waw* = 6). It represents a date. To transpose it from the era *anno mundi* to the current era, it is necessary to add 240. This brings us to 1096, the year of the First Crusade.

If Tatnu is no person, neither do its sorrows form a book. They constitute rather a library of narratives, small in size but great in substance. They are hardly literary, yet they belong to the masterpieces of literature. Their story is recorded with few ornaments of style, but their simple, poignant directness is more effective than rhetoric. Martyrdom needs no tricks of the word-artist; it tells its own tale.

The Historical Commission for the History of the Jews in Germany had but a brief career, though it has revived under the newer title of the *Gesamt-*

archiv. The Commission aimed at two ends: to introduce to Jewish notice information about the Jews scattered in Christian sources, and to make accessible to Christians facts about themselves contained in Jewish authorities. From 1887 to 1898, the Commission was actively at work, and among the books it published were two valuable volumes dealing with the martyrologies of the Jews. For the first time, these narratives were adequately edited. The pathetic records of sufferings endured in the Rhine-lands and elsewhere stand, for all time, ready to the hand of the historian.

The first moral to be extracted from these records is the certainty that war is an evil. No one can dispute the noble motives of the crusaders. The unquenchable enthusiasm which led high and low to forsake their homes and engage in eastern adventures, the unflinching courage with which the dangers of battle and the hardships and privations of wearisome campaigns were borne, the transparent singleness of purpose which animated many a soldier of the cross—all these factors tend to cover the sordid truth with a glamor of idealism and chivalry. But the wars of the Crusades were tainted with savagery, and if so what wars can be clean? The barbarities inflicted in Europe on the

Jews color with a red and gruesome haze the hero-
isms performed against Mohammedans in Asia.
War, it is said, brings to the fore some of the finest
qualities of human nature. Exactly, but the war of
man against nature calls for the exercise of the
same qualities. The heroism of the coal-mine is
as great from every point of view as the heroism
of the battlefield. And the battlefield from first
to last is the scene of human nature at its lowest as
well as at its highest. Nor is the battlefield the
whole of war. Those who persuade themselves
that war, though an evil, is not an unmixed evil,
will find in the Sorrows of Tatnu and allied books
a rather useful corrective to their complacency.

When in 1913 I re-read Neubauer and Stern's
volume (1892) and Dr. Salfeld's magnificent edition of the Nuremberg Martyrology (1898)—it
was not long before the outbreak of the European
war—I was so moved that I sent a donation to the
Peace Society. Quite a nice thing to do, some will
urge, but is it worth while, for such an end, to rake
up these miserable tales? The whole of this class
of literature was long neglected because of a similar
feeling. Stobbe, who rendered such conspicuous
service to the Jewish cause, was actuated by the
identical sentiment, when he wrote that it would be

" a grim and a thankless task " to enter fully into the sufferings of the Jews in the medieval period. But the Commission above referred to took another view; it printed the texts and circulated them in the completest detail. Now it depends entirely on the purpose with which such remorseless crimes are as remorselessly dragged to the light of day. If the desire is to revive bitterness, then it is a foul desire which ought to be crushed. And not only if this be the desire, if it prove to be the consequence, if as a result of such re-publication animosity is re-kindled, then the re-publication is to be condemned. But in the case of the Sorrows of Tatnu, neither the motive nor the consequence is of this character. Salfeld gave us his edition of these monuments of the Jewish tribulations, " den Toten zur Ehre, den Lebenden zur Lehre "; to honor the dead, to inspire the living. Neither he nor any other Jewish writer wishes to play the part of Virgil's Misenus, who was skilled in " setting Mars alight with his song " (*Martem accendere cantu*). The heroism of the sufferers, not the brutality of the aggressors, is the theme of the Jewish historian who deals with the Sorrows of Tatnu and of many another year; not the lurid glow of the bloodshed, but the white light of the martyrdom; not the pain, but the triumph over it; not the infliction, but the endurance unto and beyond death. These aspects of the story ought, indeed, to be told and retold " to honor the dead, to inspire the living."

Closely connected with this thought is another. The Commission, be it remembered, was a Jewish body, appointed by the *Deutsch-Israelitische Gemeindebund* in 1885. But Graetz was not appointed a member. (Comp. the *Memoir* in the Index Volume of Graetz's *History of the Jews*, Philadelphia, 1898, p. 78). Why did the leaders of Berlin Jewry ignore Graetz, the man who, above all others, had stirred the conscience of Europe by his vivid pictures of the medieval persecution so poignantly illustrated in the Sorrows of Tatnu? That was the very ground for excluding Graetz. There is no doubt but that Graetz's method of writing Jewish history was somewhat roughly handled at about the period named. This assault came from two sides. Treitschke, the German and Christian, attacked Graetz as anti-Christian and anti-German, and used citations from Graetz to support his propaganda of academic anti-Semitism. Certain Jews, on the other hand, felt that, though Treitschke was wrong, Graetz was too inclined to regard the world's history from a partisan and sectarian point of view. Whether or not this was the reason for the exclusion of Graetz from the Commission, what is interesting to note is the fact that the Commission, when it came to grips with the records, produced quite as emphatic an exposure of the medieval persecution as Graetz himself. It is, in brief, impossible for any student of the records to do otherwise.

The Commission included among its members some (conspicuously L. Geiger) who subsequently proved to be the strongest anti-Zionists. The duty and the desire to honor the dead for the inspiration of the living are not restricted to any one section of our community. There is nothing nationalistic or anti-nationalistic in our common sympathy with the Sorrows of Tatnu, in our common impulse to turn those sorrows to vital account in the present. In a soft age it is well to be reminded that Judaism is above all synonymous with hardihood. Thus these memories are cherished because " the blood of the martyr is the seed of the church." This magnificent thought originated with Tertullian, though the precise phrase is not his. The idea conveyed by these oft-quoted words must be carefully weighed, lest we make of it a half-truth instead of a truth. No institution is founded on its dead, it is its living upholders who alone can support it. We tell these stories of the dead, because, in their day, they, living, recognized that to save themselves men must sometimes sacrifice themselves. To pay, as the price of life, the very thing that makes life worth living is an ignoble and futile bargain. The Sorrows of Tatnu, regarded as the expression of this conviction, are converted from an elegy into a pæan. But the song is discordant unless we, who sing it, are also prepared to act it, in our own way and in our own different circumstances. *Den Toten zur Ehre, den Lebenden zur Lehre.*

PART II

Part II

IBN GEBIROL'S "ROYAL CROWN"

Authors are not invariably the best critics of their own work. Was Solomon Ibn Gebirol, who was born in Andalusia, perhaps in Malaga, in the earlier part of the eleventh century, just when he regarded as the crown of all his writings the long poem which he called the "Royal Crown" (*Keter Malkut*)? Some will always doubt his judgment. Plausibly enough, preference may be felt for several of his shorter poems, particularly "At Dawn I Seek Thee" (which Mrs. R. N. Salaman translated for the Routledge Mahzor) or "Happy the Eye that Saw these Things" (paraphrased by Mrs. Lucas in her *Jewish Year*).

Ibn Gebirol was, however, sound in his opinion. One line in the "Royal Crown" is the finest that he, or any other neo-Hebraic poet, ever wrote. Should God make visitation as to iniquity, cries Ibn Gebirol, then "from Thee I will flee to Thee." Nieto interpreted: "I will fly from Thy justice to Thy clemency." But the line needs no interpretation. In his *Confessions* (4. 9) Augustine says:

77

" Thee no man loses, but he that lets Thee go. And he that lets Thee go, whither goes he, or whither runs he, but from Thee well pleased back to Thee offended? " A great passage, but Ibn Gebirol's is greater. It is a sublime thought, and its author was inspired. He must have felt this when he named his poem. For the title comes from the Book of Esther, and the Midrash has it that, when the queen is described as donning the robes of royalty, the Scripture means to tell us that the holy spirit rested on her.

It has been said (among others, by Sachs and Steinschneider) that the " Royal Crown " is substantially a versification of Aristotle's short treatise " On the World." This is in a sense true enough. The " Royal Crown " is largely physical, and to modern readers is marred by its long paragraphs of obsolete astronomical conceptions, which go back, through the Ptolemaic system, to Aristotle. Moreover, Aristotle, in his treatise cited above, anticipated Ibn Gebirol in the motive with which he directed his ancient readers' attention to the elements and the planets. " What the pilot is in a ship, the driver in a chariot, the coryphæus in a choir, the general in an army, the lawgiver in a city—that is God in the world " (*De Mundo,* 6).

78

This saying of Aristotle is indeed Ibn Gebirol's text. But the Hebrew poet owes nothing else than the skeleton to his Greek exemplar. The style— with its superb application of biblical phrases, a method which in al-Harizi is used to raise a laugh, but in Ibn Gebirol at every turn rouses reverence— is as un-Greek as are the spiritual intensity of thought and the moral optimism of outlook.

Our Sephardic brethren were wiser than the Ashkenazim in their selections for the liturgy. Why the Ashkenazim have neglected Ibn Gebirol and ha-Levi in favor of Kalir will always remain a mystery. The Sephardim did not include all that they might have done from the Spanish poets, but the Ashkenazic Mahzor has suffered by the loss of such masterpieces as Judah ha-Levi's " Lord! unto Thee are ever manifest my inmost heart's de- sires, though unexpressed in spoken words." But most of all is our loss apparent in the omission of the " Royal Crown " from the Kol Nidre service. In Germany, the Ashkenazim have been better ad- vised. The Rödelheim Mahzor and the Michael Sachs edition both include the poem in their volumes for the Atonement Eve. Sachs (unlike de Sola) omits the astronomical sections in his fine German rendering, and wisely, for the " Royal Crown "

notably illustrates the Greek epigram: " part may
be greater than the whole." On the other hand, in
his famous *Religiöse Poesie der Juden in Spanien,*
Sachs includes the omitted cosmology. There is a
difference between our attitudes to a poem as a
work of literature and to the same poem as an invocation or prayer. Sachs the scholar refused to
mutilate the " Royal Crown," but as a liturgist
(though he printed all the Hebrew) he took liber-
ties with it.

Sachs and de Sola were not the only translators
of the " Royal Crown." In fact, to name all who
have turned Ibn Gebirol's work into modern languages would need more space than is here available. In her *Jewish Year,* Mrs. Lucas—to name
the most recent of Ibn Gebirol's translators—has
exquisitely rendered a large part of the poem. I do
not propose to quote from it, as Mrs. Lucas' book
is available at a small cost. And we shall, it is to
be hoped, not have too long to wait for Mr. Israel
Zangwill's promised rendering.

What is it that appeals to us in Ibn Gebirol's
poetry? Dr. Cowley attributes his charm to " the
youthful freshness " of his verses, " in which he
may be compared to the romantic school in France
and England in the early nineteenth century." This

same feature was also detected by al-Harizi—a better critic than poet. In fact, it was his appreciation of Ibn Gebirol's "youthful freshness" that led him to assert that the poet died before his thirties had been completed. Al-Harizi treats Ibn Gebirol's successors as his imitators. There is a large element of truth in this. One fact only need be quoted in evidence. Ibn Gebirol entitled his longest poem the "Royal Crown" (partly, no doubt, because of the frequent comparison of God to the King in the Scriptures). Now, the title "Royal Crown" passed over to designate a type of poem. We find several versifiers who later on wrote "Royal Crowns," just as we speak of an orator uttering a "Jeremiad" or a "Philippic." Heine, supreme among the modern Romantics in Germany, recognized this same freshness of inspiration in this freshest of the Spanish Hebrew poets: a pious nightingale singing in the Gothic medieval night, a nightingale whose Rose was God—these are Heine's phrases.

Gustav Karpeles again and again claims that Ibn Gebirol was the first poet thrilled by "that peculiar ferment characteristic of a modern school"—a ferment which the Germans name *Weltschmerz*. Clearly, Karpeles made a good point by showing that Schopenhauer—of whom it may be doubted whether he despised women or Jews more heartily—the apostle of *Weltschmerz,* had as a predecessor, eight centuries before his time, the despised Jew, the " Faust of Saragossa." This is another of Karpeles' epithets for Ibn Gebirol, who spent, indeed, some years in Saragossa, but had little of the Faust in him. If, however, we attribute to Ibn Gebirol the feeling of *Weltschmerz,* we must be cautious before we identify his sense of the " world's misery " with modern pessimism. Ibn Gebirol's was, no doubt, a lonely and even melancholy life. But though he often writes sadly, though he would have sympathized with William Allingham's sentiment:

> Sin we have explained away,
> Unluckily the sinners stay;

yet the final outcome of his realization of human failings and human pain was hope and not despair. And this I say not because Ibn Gebirol appreciated the humor of life as well as its miseries. It is not his humorous verses on which I should base my belief in his optimism. For I regard as the epitome, or rather, essential motive of the " Royal Crown," the lines:

Thou God, art the Light
That shall shine in the soul of the pure;
Now Thou art hidden by sin, by sin with its cloud of night.
Now Thou art hidden, but then, as over the height,
Then shall Thy glory break through the clouds that obscure,
And be seen in the mount of the Lord.

It is not pessimism but hope that speaks of the clearer vision to be won hereafter. One need not love this world less because one loves the future world more; belief in continuous growth of the soul is the most optimistic of thoughts. Critics who term Ibn Gebirol a pessimist make the common mistake of confounding despair with earnestness. Your truest optimist may be the most serious of men, just as sorrow may be at its purest, its strongest, in association with hope.

BAR HISDAI'S "PRINCE AND DERVISH"

The "moral" is a tiresome feature about certain types of allegory; we prefer that a story should tell us its own tale. Why end off with a "moral"? As Dr. Joseph Jacobs wrote in his edition of Caxton's Aesop (p. 148): "It seems absurd to give your allegory, and then, in addition, the truth which you wish to convey. Either your fable makes its point or it does not. If it does, you need not repeat your point; if it does not, you need not give your fable. To add your point is practically to confess the fear that your fable has not put it with sufficient force."

And yet it seems probable that some of the world's stories would never have been circulated so widely but for their morals. When, in the thirteenth century, Abraham Bar Hisdai, of Barcelona, produced his *Prince and Dervish,* his motive was not to tell a tale but to point a moral. He had a poor opinion of his age. Little wonder! Among the delectable episodes which he witnessed was the burning of some of the works of Maimonides by monks, instigated thereto by anti-Maimonist Jews. He made his protest. But it was not this experience that predisposed him to castigate his contemporaries. His language, in the preface to his *Prince and Dervish,* is vague. The most definite thing is its grim earnestness. His chance had come. An Arabic book had happened to fall under his notice, and it seemed to him the very thing! So he translated it into Hebrew. And beautiful Hebrew it is. Bar Hisdai was a master of the style known as rhymed prose. With him, however, it is hardly prose; it is poetry. It is not nearly so unmetrical in form as is usual in this genre. There is a lilt about his unrhythms, a regularity not so much of syllables as of stressed phrases; and these are marks of verse. Still it is prose, as one clearly perceives when Bar Hisdai, following the rules of the game, introduces snatches which are professedly poetical. Bar Hisdai, perhaps unfortunately, did more than translate. He considered his original badly arranged, he says; so he re-arranged the material. Possibly, then, he added to it stories taken from other sources. A rather piquant problem, for instance, is presented by the inclusion of a version of the parable of the sower, which in Bar Hisdai's original must have been drawn from the New Testament. Assuredly Bar Hisdai did not derive it from the latter source directly; we are quite uncertain, however, as to the indirect route by which it reached him. This is, I repeat, a little unfortunate, because it complicates the problem as to the nature of the Arabic on which he drew. The gain of the book as a collection of tales carries with it loss from the point of view of literary history.

Now what was the book which he called by the title usually rendered *Prince and Dervish?* Bar Hisdai names it " King's Son and Nazirite " (*Ben ha-Melek we-ha-Nazir*). By Nazirite he means ascetic, and Dervish is a fair reproduction which we owe to W. A. Meisel (1847). A Dervish is not the same as the biblical Nazirite, inasmuch as the former devoted himself to a much wider range of austerities than the latter. But Bar Hisdai undoubtedly intends his Nazirite to be identical with the Dervish type. How comes he to use the word in this extended sense? The answer is easily found. Bar Hisdai was a hero-worshipper, and the object of his cult was David Kimhi, the famous grammarian of Provence. Almost pathetic is Bar Hisdai's admiration for Kimhi. Now the latter, in his Hebrew dictionary (included in the *Miklol*) defines the verb *nazar* as meaning " to abstain from

eating and drinking and pleasures " (compare
Zechariah 7. 3). This was not a new idea, for the
same interpretation is given by Rashi (*loc. cit.*),
and is adumbrated in the talmudic use of the verb.
But I doubt whether Bar Hisdai would have employed the *noun* but for Kimhi's emphatic definition.

The Hebrew title, which is Bar Hisdai's own invention, well fits the contents. Briefly, these consist of a framework into which are built a number
of fables. An Indian king, fearing that his son will
become a devotee of the ascetic life, places him
(like Johnson's Rasselas) in a beautiful palace,
where he is kept ignorant of human miseries. But
he comes under the influence of a hermit (the
Nazirite), who impresses on the prince the vanity
of life, and converts him (despite the king's active
hostility) to the new way of thinking. It is in the
course of this narrative that the fables and parables
are introduced. Obviously, however, Ibn Hisdai
was much impressed by the narrative as such. " No
king nor king's son, but a slave of slaves was I
until thou didst set me free to understand and obey
God's Law "—thus does Ibn Hisdai's romance
sum up the moral at its close, the speaker being the
prince, and the one addressed the Nazirite.

A most significant point to be noted is that India is the scene of the story. In 1850 Steinschneider discovered the truth. And a surprising truth it is. The same story was known to medieval Christians as the *Romance of Barlaam and Josaphat*. But the whole is nothing more or less than an account of the life of Buddha, the great Indian saint, the founder of a religion. Jews, Mohammedans, and Christians revelled in the story without having a notion as to its original significance. Nothing so brings races and creeds together as a good tale. The folk are united by their common interest in the same lore. Mr. Zangwill, in his beautiful poem prefixed to Dr. Jacobs' edition of *Barlaam and Josaphat*, looks deeper, and finds in the general admiration for this legend a symbol of the universal identity of men's aspirations for the ideal.

> Was Barlaam truly Josaphat,
>   And Buddha truly each?
> What better parable than that
>   The unity to preach—
>
> The simple brotherhood of souls
>   That seek the highest good;
> He who in kingly chariot rolls,
>   Or wears the hermit's hood!

Bar Hisdai felt nothing of this religious cosmopolitanism. But he realized that devotion to a spiritual ideal was a lesson he might profitably present to his age in the guise of allegory.

If, however, Bar Hisdai chose the story for its moral, his readers we may be certain swallowed the moral because of the story—rather, one should say, the stories. It is remarkable that the Hebrew version is much fuller in its parables, containing, as Dr. Jacobs estimates, no less than ten not found in the other versions. Even Bar Hisdai must, after all, have been drawn to the parables as such, else why add to their number? At all events, so far as his readers went, the *Prince and Dervish* made its appeal by its stories rather than by its doctrines. And what stories they are! Several of the world's classics are in *Barlaam*, the sources of more than one of the best known dramas of later ages, some of the favorite parables of the world, immortal as human life itself. Bar Hisdai omits the caskets, which Shakespeare used in the *Merchant of Venice*, and the " Three Friends " (wealth, family, good deeds), the last of which alone accompanies a man to the grave, the plot of that famous morality play, *Everyman*. The omission is curious, for both of these tales are found in the Midrash. But Bar

Hisdai gives us the original of King Cophetua—
the beggar-maid who weds the king. Bar Hisdai
alone gives us the story of " The Robbers'
Nemesis "—the two who plot to rob the traveller,
but, envying each the other his share in the spoil,
each poisons the other rascal's food, and the traveller escapes. He also alone tells of the " Greedy
Dog," who, in his anxiety to attend two wedding
breakfasts on the same day, misses both. But we
cannot go through all. One other, found only in
Bar Hisdai, is thus summarized by Dr. Jacobs:

A king, hunting, invites a shepherd to eat with him in the heat
of the day:

Shepherd: I cannot eat with thee, for I have already promised
another greater than thee.

King: Who is that?

Shepherd: God, who has invited me to fast.

King: But why fast on such a hot day?

Shepherd: I fast for a day still hotter than this.

King: Eat to-day, fast to-morrow.

Shepherd: Yes, if you will guarantee that I shall see to-morrow.

Such stories are sure to see many a to-morrow.
And among the best records of them, among the
most notable repertoires of the world's wit and
wisdom, Bar Hisdai's *Prince and Dervish* has a
sure place.

THE SARAJEVO HAGGADAH

Sarajevo, scene of the crime which led to the outbreak of the European War, has its more pleasant associations. The place is forever connected with the history of Jewish art, and in particular with the illumination of the Passover Home-Service or Haggadah.

Wonderful in the old sense of the word—that is to say, astonishing—is the fact that, though the Sarajevo Haggadah was printed a good many years ago (in 1898), there have been no imitations. The splendid Russian publication of Stassof and Günzburg certainly came more recently (1905), but it cannot be compared with the Hungarian work of Müller and Von Schlossar. "L'Ornement Hebreu" is scrappy; the "Haggada von Sarajevo," though it includes many selections from other manuscripts, is a unity. In one point, however, the Russians were right. For a Jewish illuminative art we must look rather to masoretic margins than to full-page pictures. The former must be characteristically Jewish, the latter, though found in Hebrew liturgies and scrolls, are often non-Jewish types. This is clearly shown by the famous picture in the Sarajevo Haggadah wherein is probably depicted the Deity resting after the work of creation. But for all that, the Sarajevo book must remain supreme as an introduction to Jewish art, so long as it continues to be the only completely reproduced Hebrew illuminated manuscript of the Middle Ages.

One would like to hope that it will not always retain this unique position. The Crawford Haggadah (now in the Rylands Library, Manchester) is certainly older, and, in my judgment, finer. It is true that the editors of the Sarajevo manuscript claim that theirs is the most ancient illuminated Haggadah extant. They admit that the *text* of the Crawford Haggadah is older by at least half-a-century, but assert that the full-page pictures belong to the fifteenth century, thus falling two centuries after the text. I altogether contest this statement. But even if it were conceded, nevertheless the beauty of the Crawford Haggadah consists just in the text, in the beautiful margins, full of spirited grotesques and arabesques, no doubt (like the Sarajevo manuscript itself) produced in Spain under strong North French influence. Mr. Frank Haes executed a complete photograph of the Crawford manuscript, and it ought undoubtedly to be published. As I write, I have before me two pages of Mr. Haes' reproduction—the *dayyenu* passage; nothing in Jewish illuminated work can approach this, unless it be the rather inferior, but very beautiful, British Museum manuscript of the same type. The editors of the Sarajevo Haggadah were ill-advised in omitting to repoduce the whole of the text of their precious original. It is in the text that the genuine excellence of the Jewish manuscripts is to be found.

But the Sarajevo Haggadah gives us too much that is delightful for us to cavil over what it does not give. Here we have, in the full-page drawings, depicted the history of Israel from the days of the Creation, the patriarchal story, Joseph in Egypt, the coming of Moses, the Egyptian plagues, the exodus, the revelation, the temple that is yet to be. Very interesting is the picture of a synagogue. This late thirteenth (or early fourteenth) century sketch evidently knows nothing of the now most usual ornament of a synagogue—the tablets of the decalogue over the ark. On this subject, however, I have written elsewhere, and as my remarks have been published, I can pass over this point on the present occasion. I have mentioned above the striking attempt to depict the Deity, but it is equally noteworthy that in the revelation picture no such attempt is made. Into Moses' ear a horn conveys the inspired message; but the artist does not introduce God. At least, one hopes not. We prefer to regard the figure at the top of the mountain as Moses, and it is not difficult to account in that case for the figure standing rather lower up the hill, also holding the tablets. We must assume that this under figure is Aaron, though it is not recorded that he received the tablets from his brother. There is another possibility. In the medieval illuminations it was a frequent device to express various parts of a continuous scene in the same drawing. Thus the Sarajevo artist may have intended to show us Moses in two positions, and though the method lacks perspective, the effect is not devoid of realistic power. That this is probably the true explanation of the Sinai scene is suggested by another—Jacob's dream. Here we see Jacob asleep (with one angel descending, another higher up ascending the ladder—the artist has not troubled himself with the problem as to how the angels contrived to cross one another). But we also see Jacob awake, *on the same picture,* for he is anointing the Beth-el stone and converting it into an altar.

Certainly the drawings, sadly though they lack proportion, are realistic. Especially is this true of the portrayal of Lot's wife transformed into a pillar of salt. Disproportionate in size, for she is taller than Sodom's loftiest pinnacles, yet the artist has succeeded in suggesting the gradual stiffening of her figure: we *see* her becoming rigid before our eyes. There is clearly much that modern artists might learn from these medieval gropings towards realism. Some artists have already learned much. It is quite obvious, for instance, that Burne-Jones must have steeped himself in the suggestive mysticism of the Middle Ages before he painted his marvellous Creation series. The parallel between his series and the series in the Sarajevo Haggadah is undeniable. Though he never saw this Haggadah, he was well acquainted with similar work in the Missals. Just as Keats evolved his theory as to the identity of truth and beauty from a Greek vase, so the pre-Raphaelites re-told on vases what they read in their moments of communion with the medieval spirit.

And this leads to what must be my last word now on this Hebrew masterpiece. If a Burne-Jones can thus imitate, why not a Solomon or a Lilien? The latter has now produced a series of illustrations to

the Bible, but we want something less coldly classic,
something more warmly symbolic. It was indicated above, with regret, that Mr. Haes' photo-
graphs of the Crawford Haggadah are still
unpublished. But over and above reproductions
of extant works, we need new works. Now the
Jewish artist who illustrates a Bible ought not to
be content to illustrate anything but a Hebrew text.
And if a Bible be for several reasons out of the
question, why should we not have a new Haggadah, written by a living Jewish artist, who shall,
from a close study of olden models, do for us what
Burne-Jones did?—that is, extract from the mysticism of a by-gone age those abiding truths which
our contemporary age demands of its art.

A PIYYUT BY BAR ABUN

Not every one named Solomon was Ibn Gebirol.
The medieval poets often signed their verses by an
acrostic. Now, when a poem has the signature of
a particular name, the natural tendency has been
to ascribe it to the most famous bearer of the name.
Of all the poetical Solomons, Ibn Gebirol was, beyond question, the greatest. Zunz was the first
who clearly discriminated between the various
authors called by the same personal name. The
hymn "Judge of all the Earth" (*Shofet Kol
ha-Arez*) was certainly by a Solomon; Zunz iden-
tifies him with the Frenchman Solomon, son of
Abun. This Solomon is described as " the youth "
(*ha-Na'ar*), perhaps in the sense that there was a
" senior " poet of the same name. According to
Zunz, again, Solomon bar Abun's period of active
authorship lay presumably between the years 1170
and 1190. (*Literaturgeschichte der synagogalen
Poesie*, p. 311.)

Of all his works the piyyut we are considering is
by far the most popular. A spirited rendering of
the poem, by Mrs. R. N. Salaman, may be found

in the Routledge Mahzor so ably edited in part by her father. (See the *Day of Atonement,* morning service, page 86.) Three stanzas had, however, long before been published by Mrs. Henry Lucas in her *Jewish Year* (p. 44). Some years ago the same gifted translator completed the whole of the hymn, and her version is now printed here in full. I say " in full," though there is a longer form of the poem containing *six* verses. Zunz, however, only assigns *five* verses to the original, and the sixth verse is probably an unauthorized addition. It repeats the idea of the second verse, and also disturbs the acrostic signature. This piyyut or hymn must have been designed for the New Year. True, in the only " German " Mahzor known to many, the poem is included among the Selihot for the Day of Atonement. Though, however, Solomon bar Abun's masterpiece is fairly suitable for the Fast, it is not altogether appropriate for that occasion. The " German " rite, accordingly, is well advised when it also employs the piyyut for the day before New Year. Even more to be commended are those liturgies—the Yemenite and some of the " Spanish "—which appoint the poem for the New Year itself. That is obviously its true place. With its opening phrase, " Judge of all the earth," the hymn declares its character. It was written for the Day of Judgment—that is, for the New Year's Day. Moreover, these initial words are taken from Abraham's intercession for the sinners of Sodom (Genesis 18. 25), and this is preceded by the announcement of Isaac's birth, an incident which one form of the Jewish tradition connects with the New Year. It must be remembered in general that prayers intended originally for one occasion were often transferred to others. Thus the *Alenu* prayer, now used every day, was at first composed for the New Year *Musaf*.

Let us now turn to the poem itself, which, as already stated, is reproduced in the version from the hand of Mrs. Lucas.

> Judge of the earth, who wilt arraign
>   The nations at thy judgment seat,
> With life and favor bless again
>   Thy people prostrate at thy feet.
> And mayest Thou our morning prayer
> Receive, O Lord, as though it were
> The offering that was wont to be
> Brought day by day continually.
>
> Thou who art clothed with righteousness,
>   Supreme, exalted over all—
> How oft soever we transgress,
>   Do Thou with pardoning love recall

Those who in Hebron sleep: and let
Their memory live before Thee yet,
Even as the offering unto Thee
Offered of old continually.

O Thou, whose mercy faileth not,
   To us Thy heavenly grace accord;
Deal kindly with Thy people's lot,
   And grant them life, our King and Lord.
Let Thou the mark of life appear
Upon their brow from year to year,
As when were daily wont to be
The offerings brought continually.

Restore to Zion once again
   Thy favor and the ancient might
And glory of her sacred fane,
   And let the son of Jesse's light
Be set on high, to shine always,
Far shedding its perpetual rays,
Even as of old were wont to be
The offerings brought continually.

Trust in God's strength, and be ye strong,
   My people, and His law obey,
Then will He pardon sin and wrong,
   Then mercy will his wrath outweigh;
Seek ye His presence, and implore
His countenance for evermore.
Then shall your prayers accepted be
As offerings brought continually.

100

When this is sung or declaimed to the appropriate melody (on which the Rev. F. L. Cohen has much of interest to say in the *Jewish Encyclopedia,* xi, 306), the solemn effect of words and music is profound. The refrain (from Numbers 28. 23), recalls the close association which, even while the sanctuary stood, subsisted between temple sacrifices and synagogue prayers. Since the loss of the shrine, prayer has fulfilled the double function. There are only one or two phrases that need elucidation. In the second stanza the words " Those who in Hebron sleep " refer to those of the patriarchs who were buried in Hebron, in the cave of Machpelah. The appeal is made to the merits of the fathers, a subject on which the reader will do well to consult the Rev. S. Levy's essay in his volume entitled " Original Virtue." In the third stanza occurs the phrase " mark of life." This is derived from the ninth chapter of Ezekiel—those bearing the " mark " are, in the prophet's vision, to live amid the general destruction. Life—the merciful verdict of the Judge, quite as much as the judgment itself—is the note of the New Year liturgy. This poem strikes both notes with undeniable power.

ISAAC'S LAMP AND JACOB'S WELL

To have one's Hebrew book turned into the current speech, to have it read part by part in the synagogue by one's fellows as a substitute for sermons, is not a common experience. Isaac Aboab enjoyed this honor. His *Menorat ha-Maor,* or *Candelabrum of the Light,* written in Spain somewhere about the year 1300, according to Zunz, or in France a little before 1400, according to Dr. Efros, became one of the most popular books of the late Middle Ages.

Well it deserved the favor which it won. The Talmud, said Aboab, may be used by the learned in their investigations of law. But for the masses, he felt, it has also a message. Aboab was the first (unless Dr. Efros be right in claiming this honor for Israel Alnaqua) to pick out from the Talmud and Midrash, from the gaonic and even later rabbinic writings, passages of every-day morals, ethical principles, secular and religious wisdom. Aboab's work was not, however, a mere hap-hazard collection of detached sentences and maxims.

Zedner (*Catalogue*, p. 381), does not hesitate to term it a " System of Moral Laws as explained in the Talmud." Indeed, the book is surprisingly systematic. The first, or among the first, of its kind, it is also a most conspicuous example of the due ordering of materials.

The very title, also used by Alnaqua, and derived from Numbers 4. 9, was an inspiration. It conveys the idea of " illumination," than which no idea penetrates deeper into the spiritual life. Fancifully enough, Aboab continues the metaphor into the main divisions of his book. The *Menorah* (Candelabrum) of the Pentateuch branched out into seven lamps, and so Aboab's book is divided also into " Seven Lamps." It is strange that he did not carry the metaphor further. He divides each of his " Lamps " into Parts and Chapters, with a Prologue and an Epilogue to each Lamp. The fourth chapter of Zechariah might have given him " olive-trees " for his Prologues, " bowls " for his Epilogues, and " pipes " for his Parts, while " wicks " might have served instead of Chapters. In point of fact, the " Seven Wicks " was the title chosen by Aboab's epitomator, Moses Frankfurt, when he constructed a reduced copy of Aboab's *Candelabrum* (Amsterdam, 1721).

To return to Aboab's original work, Lamp I deals with Retribution, Desire, and Passion, Honor, and High-place—the motives and ends of moral conduct. In Lamp II is unfolded the rabbinic teaching on Irreverence, Hypocrisy, Profanation of the Name, Frivolity as distinct from Joy— the causes which impede morality. Then, in Lamp III—the largest Lamp of all the seven—we have morality at work practically, and are instructed as to the worth of religious exercises, charitable life, social and domestic virtue, justice in man's dealings with his fellows. Next, in Lamp IV, is unfolded the duty and the great reward of studying the Law, as a beautiful corollary to the love and fear of God. Far-reaching in its analysis of the human soul is Lamp V, on Repentance. Lamp VI may be described as presenting the good Rule for body and mind, the amenities of life as shown in character. Or perhaps one might better put it that this section shows us how to be gentlemen, clean, wholesome, considerate. Then Lamp VII completes the whole. It sets out the ideals of Humility and Modesty, virtues which are the end, nay, the beginning also, of the noblest human possibilities, for these virtues are first in those wherein man may imitate God.

Appropriately, Aboab follows up his glorious eulogy of Humility with a full confession of his own shortcomings. He knows that his compilation is imperfect. " Some things I have omitted," he explains, " because I have never read them; others because I have forgotten them." " Some passages I left out," he goes on, " as too abstruse for general reading, others as alien to the purpose of my book, others again because liable to misunderstanding, and liable to do more harm than good." Wise man! Unfortunately not every imitator of Aboab has displayed the same excellent judgment. The olden Jewish literature is so abundantly full of beauties that it is an ill-service to repeat the few things of lesser value. Aboab's *Candelabrum of the Light* is in this respect superior to its great rival, Ibn Habib's *Well of Jacob*. Up to half-a-century ago the two books must have run each other very close as regards the number of editions; more recently Ibn Habib's book (the *'En Ya'akob*) has probably surged ahead. Readers may be reminded of the difference in method. Ibn Habib takes the talmudic tractates one by one, and extracts from each its *haggadic* elements. There is no attempt at any other order than that of the Talmud. The *Well of Jacob*, moreover, includes everything, the folk-lore as well as the ethics. To the student, Ibn Habib's service was greater than Aboab's; the relation is reversed from the point of view of the man or woman in search of vital religion.

The *Well of Jacob,* it must be allowed, is in itself almost as good a title as that which Aboab chose. Ibn Habib himself seems to have used the Hebrew word *'En* rather in the sense of " Substance " or " Essence "—his work reproduced the " Essence " of the talmudic Haggadah. But *Jacob's Well,* as the Midrash has it, was the source whence was drawn the Holy Spirit. Despite my personal preference for Aboab's *Menorah,* it must be freely acknowledged that many generations have quaffed from Ibn Habib's reservoir fine spiritual draughts. And still quaff. For just as Aboab's *Lamp* still shines, so Jacob's *Well* has not yet run dry.

Over and above the similarity of contents, with all the dissimilarity of method, there is another reason why one thinks of the works of Aboab and Ibn Habib together. Though Aboab wrote considerably before Ibn Habib, their books appeared for the first time in print almost simultaneously. Ibn Habib's book came out as the author compiled it; in point of fact it was the son who

completed the publication, because Jacob Ibn
Habib died while the earlier sections of his work
were passing through the press. If, as seems probable, the *Lamp* was first kindled in 1511, or 1514,
and the *Well* began to pour its fertilizing streams
in 1516, Aboab had the start; but these dates are
uncertain. All that we can state with confidence is
that both books appeared in print quite early in
the sixteenth century, not later than 1516. The
earliest editions of both books are scarce, and from
a simple cause. Few copies have survived because
the owners of the copies *wore them out*. Read and
re-read, thumbed by many hands, by " the Jewish
woman, the workman, the rank and file of Israel,"
the copies were used up by those who treated books
as something to hold in the hand and not to keep on
a shelf out of reach. My own edition of the *Candelabrum,* that of Amsterdam (1739), boasts
justly of the excellent paper on which it is printed.
None the less does this copy, too, show signs of
frequent perusal. The best books were the worst
preserved, because they were the best treated.
What better treatment of a book can there be than
to read it so often that its pages no longer hold together, its margins fray, and its title-page suffers
mutilation?

107

"LETTERS OF OBSCURE MEN"

Does ridicule kill? If it did, then, as fools are always with us, folly would ever possess the flavor of novelty. And yet to-day's fool looks and does very much the same as yesterday's, even though wise men laughed their fill at the latter. Folly, one rather must admit, is immortal. Wise men come and wise men go, but fools go on forever. Wisdom can at most make the fool look foolish for a while.

At rare intervals, however, history offers an example of the slaying power of satire. Idolatry was killed by ridicule. Some people—among them Renan, who ought to have known better—deny to ancient Israel a sense of humor. But who can doubt that the most effective of the attacks on idolatry were Elijah's sarcastic invective against the Baal of the populace (I Kings 18. 27) and Isaiah's grim yet droll picture of the carpenter taking some timber and using part of it to bake his bread and the rest to make his god (Isaiah 44. 15)? It is far from our purpose to recite the success, in after ages, of less inspired efforts by satirists. Satire has been termed the "chief refuge of the weak"; it has certainly been a weapon by which one, standing alone, has often equalized the odds against him. It would be delightful to give illustrations of the methods by which the various warriors of the pen have used their sword: to contrast a pagan Juvenal and a Hebrew Kalonymos—both writing in Rome, but with more than a millennium between them— or to revel in the feats of Rabelais' *Gargantua* (1534), Cervantes' *Don Quixote* (1605), Pascal's *Provincial Letters* (1656), and Voltaire's eighteenth century *Candide*. We are now concerned with a work and a group of authors who first made Europe laugh in 1515. Ulrich von Hutten and his associates, in their "Letters of Obscure Men" (*Epistolae Obscurorum Virorum*), did just the right thing at the right moment. What they attempted, what they accomplished, will now be told. Cervantes, tilting against the wearisome nonsense of the later romances of chivalry, Pascal exposing— even though he did it unfairly— the dangers of casuistry, Voltaire plumbing the shallow optimism of Leibnitz, served good ends. But far higher than these was the cause triumphantly upheld by the *Letters of Obscure Men*. The cause was humanism, another name for intellectual freedom and width of view.

Briefly put, at the crisis in the fortune of the new learning in Europe, when the struggle was at its sharpest between ignorance and enlightenment, the vindication of the Talmud became identified with the overthrow of intellectual bigotry. Pfefferkorn wished to burn the Talmud. He was a shady character, and from his first condition as a bad Jew became, in Erasmus' phrase, a worse Christian ("ex scelerato Judaeo sceleratissimus Christianus"). Pfefferkorn hurled against his former coreligionists the usual missiles of abuse. Why is it that the converted Jew is so often a bitter assailant of Judaism? Some answer that it is because the renegade must prove that he forsook something execrable. Others would have it that intrinsic vileness of character is responsible. But is it not more probable that apostate virulence is due simply to ignorance? And this is the more obnoxious when the animosity takes the form of an attack on literature. "Ignorance, which in matters of morals extenuates the crime, is itself, in matters of literature, a crime of the first order." So said Joubert, and the remark can be freely illustrated from the Pfefferkorns. When a real scholar leaves the synagogue, he is rarely among the anti-Semites. Daniel Chwolson and Paul Cassel in their career as

Judæo-Christians were champions of the Jewish cause against such very libels as a Pfefferkorn would circulate. At the beginning of the sixteenth century the defence of Judaism was in equally scholarly hands.

But it was not on Jews, whether by race or religion, that reliance was then placed. Reuchlin— as all the world knows—saw no reason why the Talmud should be condemned, and he expressed his opinion in clear terms. Reuchlin, be it remembered, was the most learned German of his age. " By a singular combination of taste and talents this remarkable man excelled at once as a humanist and a man of affairs, as a jurist and a mystic, and, above all, as a pioneer among Orientalists, so that it has been said of him, enthusiastically but not unjustly, that he was the ' first who opened the gates of the East, unsealed the Word of God, and unveiled the sanctuary of Hebrew wisdom.' " (This sentence is quoted from the Introduction to Mr. Francis Griffin Stokes' admirable Latin and English edition of the *Letters,* to which I cordially commend my readers.) Pfefferkorn rallied to his side the whole force of the Dominican organization. The issue was long uncertain.

111

Truth is usually unable to meet falsehood on equal terms; the genuine, for the most part, cannot soil its hands with the foul ammunition of imposture. Sometimes, however, truth is less squeamish. And so, when Pfefferkorn was engaged in slinging slime at Reuchlin, there was suddenly hurled at his own person an avalanche of mud, under which he and his party sank buried from heel to head. The *Letters* are remorseless in their personalities. But if it be impossible to deny their cruelty and even their occasional coarseness, yet their fame depends less on these scurrilous incidentals than on the essential truth on which they are based.

It is the highest merit of satire that it shall not be too obvious. Many who read *Gulliver's Travels* enjoy it as a tale, and may not even realize that Swift was lampooning the society and institutions of his day. So long as this element in satire is not too subtle, it adds enormously to the merit of the performance. One recalls such stories as the *Descent of Man,* by Edith Wharton. The hero of that tale is an eminent zoologist, who is moved by the popularity of pseudo-scientific defences of religion to publish an elaborate skit. But he is so successful in concealing his object, that his " Vital Thing " is mistaken for a supreme example of the very type of work he is lashing. The *Letters of Obscure Men* avoided this danger. They hit the happy mean. They purported to be written by one obscurantist to another, and while the educated at once saw through the dodge, the illiterate (including Pfefferkorn himself) took them seriously. Within a few months of the appearance of the first series of the *Letters,* Sir Thomas More (in 1616) wrote to Erasmus: " It does one's heart good to see how delighted everybody is with the ' Epistolae Obscurorum Virorum '; the learned are tickled by their humor, while the unlearned deem their teachings of serious worth." The foes of humanism— the new learning—are left to expose themselves, in the confidential correspondence which members of the gang are made to carry on in the most excruciatingly funny dog-Latin. As Bishop Creighton put it, they are made to " tell their own story, to wander round the narrow circle of antiquated prejudices which they mistook for ideas, display their grossness, their vulgarity, their absence of aim, their laborious indolence, their lives unrelieved by any touch of nobility." No wonder Europe laughed, as it did in the following century at the self-revelation of obscurants in Pascal's *Provincial Letters,* obviously inspired by the work before us. (Compare Stokes, *Epistolae,* etc., pp. xlvi, xlix). It is not the least amusing feature in the comedy that Richard Steele actually regarded the *Letters of Obscure Men* as the correspondence between " some profound blockheads " who wrote " in honor of each other, and for their mutual information in each other's absurdities." (Stokes, p. viii).

This fate—of being taken seriously—befell, in a particularly amusing way, what is perhaps the most amusing of all the *Letters.* I refer to the second epistle in the first series. " Magister Johannes Pelzer " sends his greeting to " Magister Ortwin Gratius," and asks help on a matter which gives him " great searchings of heart." He tells Ortwin how, being lately at a Frankfort fair, he took off his cap and saluted two men, who seemed reputable and looked like Doctors of Divinity. But his companion then nudged him and cried: " God-a-mercy, what doest thou? Those fellows are Jews." Magister Pelzer goes on to argue with delicious seriousness as to the nature of his sin, and begs his correspondent's help to decide whether it was " mortal or venial, episcopal or papal." Now when Schudt came to compile his farrago of attacks on the Jews, he actually included this Frankfort inci-

dent as an authentic example of "Jewish inso-
lence." It was indeed painful for such as Schudt
to be unable to discern any difference between a Jew
and a gentleman.

How the authors of the *Letters* would have
chuckled over Steele and Schudt! Reuchlin had
struck a decisive blow in behalf of the Jewish contribution to European culture. The *Letters* drove
the blow home. But, after all, the fools were not
permanently suppressed. No, ridicule rarely slays
folly outright. It scotches the snake, and then in a
favorable environment the reptile revives. Just
as folly is perennial, so should the lash be kept in
constant repair. Anti-Semitism ought not to be
allowed to go on its way in our age unscathed by
ridicule. We badly need a new Ulrich von Hutten
to give us a modern series of Letters of Obscure
Men.

DE ROSSI'S " LIGHT OF THE EYES "

Towards dusk, on a mid-November Friday in the year 1570, Azariah de Rossi descended from his own apartments to those of his married daughter. It was in Ferrara, and for some hours past earth-tremblings had made people anxious. Within an hour of his lucky visit to his child De Rossi's abode was wrecked.

To this earthquake, as Zunz suggested in 1841 (*Kerem Hemed,* vol. v, p. 135), we owe the first attempt by a Jew to investigate critically, and with the aid of secular research, the history of Jewish literature. De Rossi had a fine command of Latin, and though he was less at home with Greek, he had a good working knowledge of it. After the earthquake, he left his home, and took refuge in a village south of the Po. A Christian scholar, a neighbor in the new settlement, was diverting his mind from the recent disturbing calamities, by perusing the Letter of Aristeas. There is a rare charm in the scene that followed. Finding some difficulties in the Letter, the Christian turned to the Jew, suggesting that they should consult the Hebrew text.

116

But De Rossi was, to his chagrin, compelled to admit that there *was* no Hebrew text! Such a lamentable deficiency need not, however, continue. In less than three weeks De Rossi had translated the Letter into Hebrew, and with that act the modern study of Jewish records by Jews opens.

Chroniclers were once upon a time fond of contrasting the physique and the intellect of the worthies of former ages. Those were the days, one might almost say, of " kakogenics," if our own is the era of eugenics. So we read of De Rossi that though " well-born " by ancestry, he was " ill-born " in person. Graetz somewhat overcolors the record when he writes of De Rossi thus: " Feeble, yellow, withered, and afflicted with fever, he crept about like a dying man." At all events, he was thin and short, and neglectful of his bodily health. Yet he was not quite the weakling Graetz presents, for he lived to the age of sixty-four (1514-1578). Moreover, he assures us, giving full details of the diet and treatment, that he was thoroughly cured of the malaria, of the ravages of which Italian Jews so frequently complain. As to his " family," that was old enough. The legend ran that four of the families settled by Titus in Rome survived into the Middle Ages; the stock of the De Rossis

117

(*min ha-adummim*) belonged to one of the famous quartette. The other three were the Mansi, de Pomis, and Adolescentoli groups.

This was the man who created modern Jewish " science "—to use the term so beloved of our Continental brethren. De Rossi's great work appeared as a quarto in November, 1573 (some date it 1574). It was well printed in the pretty square Hebrew type for which Mantua is famous. The author called it *Meor 'Enayim,* that is, " Light of the Eyes." It was, indeed, an illuminant. Graetz summarily asserts that " the actual results of this historical investigation, for the most part, have proved unsound." Assuredly many of De Rossi's statements are no longer accepted. He was the father of criticism, yet he was often himself uncritical. In his chapter on the antiquity of the Hebrew language, for instance, he remarks: " I have seen among many ancient coins, belonging to David Finzi of Mantua, a silver coin on which, on the obverse, is a man's head round which is inscribed ' King Solomon ' in Hebrew square letters, while the reverse bears a figure of the temple with the Hebrew legend ' Temple of Solomon.' " As Zunz observes, this coin must have been a modern fabrication. In many other points De Rossi erred.

But some of the " mistakes " for which he is blamed are not his but his critics'. Zunz, like Graetz, had little patience with the Zohar. The literature of the Kabbalah was to both these great scholars " false and corrupt." At this date we are much more inclined to treat the Kabbalah with respect. De Rossi has been justified by later research. Then, again, Zunz categorically includes among De Rossi's blunders his acceptance of the Letter of Aristeas as genuine. But in the year 1904 Mr. H. St. J. Thackeray, in the preface to his new English translation of the Letter, asserts " recent criticism has set in the direction of rehabilitating the story, or at any rate part of it." Here, one can have no hesitation in claiming, De Rossi was right, and his critics wrong.

It is pleasing to be able to make this last assertion. The Letter of Aristeas purports to tell the story how the Greek translation of the Pentateuch was made in Alexandria. We are not now concerned with the story itself. But, as we have already seen, it was this Letter which induced De Rossi to write his book. The book, after a short section on the Ferrara earthquake, in which the author collects much Jewish and non-Jewish seismological lore, goes straight to Aristeas. Now,

it would be a somewhat unfortunate fact if Jewish
criticism began with the acceptance of a forgery, if
the father of all our modern scholars (including
Zunz himself) had started off with a bad critical
mistake. We are spared this anomaly, for though
Aristeas may not be as old as it claims (the third
century B. C. E.), it is demonstrably older than
its assailants made it out to be. De Rossi is far
nearer the truth than Graetz. Of course, we do
not now turn to De Rossi for our critical nourish-
ment. Though editions of the *Meor 'Enayim*
continued to appear as late as 1866 (in fact one of
the author's books appeared for the first time in
London in 1854), his works are substantially obsolete. For this reason I am not attempting any close
account of their contents.

But while it is antiquated in this sense, it is a
book of the class that can never become unimpor-
tant. For let us realize what De Rossi accomplished. In the first place he directed Jewish
attention to the Jewish literature preserved or written in Greek. He re-introduced Philo to Jewish
notice; not very accurately, it is true, yet he *did*
re-introduce him. Secondly, he showed how much
was to be derived from a study of non-Jewish
sources. No one, after De Rossi, has for a moment

thought it possible to deal with Jewish history entirely from Jewish records. Every available material must be drawn on if we are to construct a sound edifice. It is a just verdict of Graetz's that De Rossi's "power of reconstruction was small." But he showed subsequent generations how to build. De Rossi, finally, was not one who regarded Jewish literature merely as the subject matter for research. He was intensely interested in it for its own sake. He was a poet as well as a historian. And this he shows both by his whole style and outlook as well as by the Hebrew and Italian verses that he wrote. He was, indeed, known both as Azariah and as Bonajuto, the latter being the Italian equivalent. Let us end with this fact: the same man, who inaugurated modern Jewish criticism, added some notable hymns to the synagogue prayer-book.

GUARINI AND LUZZATTO

An aristocrat all his life, Guarini was out of place in the court life of Ferrara. He spent his vigor in a vain attempt to accommodate himself to the sixteenth century Italian conditions. Then, broken in strength and fortune, he retired to produce his dramatic masterpiece. Not that the *Pastor Fido* can be truly termed dramatic. It is much more of a lyric. But just as Banquo, himself no king, was the father of kings, so Guarini, of little consequence as a dramatist, begot famous dramas. For the *Faithful Shepherd* deeply influenced European drama throughout the two centuries which followed its publication in 1590.

The Hebraic muse owed much to Guarini. Moses Hayyim Luzzatto (1707-1747) has been the only writer of Hebrew plays whose work counts in the literary sense. Luzzatto derived his whole dramatic inspiration from Guarini. Let no one question this assertion without first comparing *La-Yesharim Tehillah* and *Migdal 'Oz* with the *Pastor Fido*. The characters and scenes, and even more, the style, are closely alike. Nor is this latter fact wonderful. John Addington Symonds describes Guarini's work as "a masterpiece of diction, glittering and faultless, like a bas-relief of hard Corinthian bronze." Luzzatto produces the same effect in his Hebrew imitation, using a similar metre as well as similar dramatic conventions. In imitating, however, he re-interprets. Guarini's play is sometimes gross, it is never truly rustic. But a Hebrew poet, moved by such models as the Song of Songs, better knew how to be sensuous with purity; grossness must be anti-pathetic to him. On the other hand, Hebrew poetry is genuinely rustic. The biblical shepherd, whether in scriptural history or romance, is the most beloved of heroes. Some of the great characters of the Bible are shepherds: Abraham, Moses, David, Amos, Shulammith—but why pile up instances? It is obvious that a Hebrew poet, adopting a rural background for a lyrical drama, must inevitably write with sincerity. He could not, at the same time, fail to write with delicacy. Luzzatto took much from Guarini, but he both refined and adorned what he borrowed.

Yet, though it is because of Luzzatto that I am writing of Guarini, nevertheless, Guarini, and not Luzzatto, is my present subject. So I will re-tell

for the reader the story of the *Pastor Fido*. Not
that it is an easy task. Guarini, who influenced the
late Elizabethans, shared, with the best of the latter, the inordinate fancy for complicated plots.
Plot is entangled within plot, until we lose sight of
the main theme. Luzzatto—I find it impossible to
keep the Hebrew out!—here simplifies. He hardly
gives us a story at all; he provides an allegory,
eking out Guarini with Midrash. In the process of
disentangling Guarini's intricacies, he somewhat
sacrifices the chief merit of his Italian model.
Luzzatto's *dramatis personae* are almost abstrac-
tions; they remind us of the figures in morality
plays. A Luzzatto drama more resembles *Everyman* than it does *As You Like it*. Of Guarini, on
the other hand, it may be said, that though he means
his characters to represent types, he draws them as
individuals. Silvio, to adopt Mr. Symond's sum-
maries, is " cold and eager "; Mirtillo " tender
and romantic." Corisca's " meretricious arts " contrast with and enhance Amarillis's " pure affection "; Dorinda is " shameless." The dramatist,
however, be he Luzzatto or Guarini, writes with a
distinct tendency. His aim is to set up the country
life and the country girl as essentially superior to
the city varieties. This *motive* is as old as satire,

and as young as the " verses of society." Austin
Dobson's Phyllida is all that is sweet and natural,
she is a foil to the artificiality of the " ladies of
St. James's." Guarini enjoys the honor not of
creating the mood, but of bringing it into new
vogue.

But I am still keeping from the story. The
scene is Arcadia. Yearly the inhabitants must
sacrifice a young maiden to Diana. Diana had suffered through the perfidy of Lucrina; but the
Oracle declares:

> Your Woes, Arcadians! never shall have End,
>   Till Love shall two conjoin of heavenly Race,
> And till a faithful Shepherd shall amend,
>   By matchless Zeal, Lucrina's old Disgrace.

Montano, the priest of Diana, seeks, therefore,
to join in marriage his only son, Silvio, to the noble
nymph, Amarillis, descended from Pan. But
Silvio thought more of hunting than of love. The
young shepherd, Mirtillo, becomes enamored of
Amarillis, and she of him. The artful Corisca,
desiring the shepherd for herself, charges Amarillis
with infidelity—she is betrothed, though not
wedded, to Silvio. Amarillis is sentenced to death.
Mirtillo offers himself, and is accepted, as her substitute. Led to the—fatal, not the bridal—altar,

Mirtillo's identity is discovered. The shepherd is Montano's son. Let us read the rest in the terms of the " argument " (as given in the 1782 English version) : " On which Occasion, the true Father, bewailing that it should fall to his lot to execute the law on his own blood—(for to Montano, as priest, the office of carrying out the sacrificial rite belonged)—is by Tirenio, a blind soothsayer, clearly satisfied by the interpretation of the Oracle itself, that it was not only opposite to the will of the gods that this victim should be sacrificed, but moveover that the happy period (*i. e.,* end) was now come to the woes of Arcadia, which had been predicted by the sacred Voice, and from which, as every circumstance now strongly corresponded, they concluded that Amarillis could not be, nor ought to be, the spouse of any other than Mirtillo. And as a little previous to this, Silvio, thinking to wound a wild beast, had pierced Dorinda, who had been exceedingly distressed by the slight he had shown to her violent passion for him, but whose wonted savageness was changed by this accident and softened into compassion—after her wound was healed, which at first was thought mortal, and after Amarillis was become the spouse of Mirtillo, he too became now enamoured of Dorinda, and married her; by means of these events, so happy and so extraordinary, Corisca is at length convinced of and confesses her guilt, and, having implored pardon and obtained it from the loving couple, her perturbed spirit now pacified and satiated with the Follies of the World, she determines to change her Course of Life." The play ends with the wedding chorus for the hero and heroine (Luzzatto, too, wrote his plays for marriage celebrations). In words very like those used by Luzzatto, Guarini's shepherds sing to Mirtillo and Amarillis:

> O happy pair!
> Who have in Sorrow sown, and reap'd in Joy,
> How hath your bitter share of grief's alloy
> Now sweetened and confirmed your present bliss!
> And may ye learn from this,
> Blind, feeble mortals! to distinguish right
> What are true ills, and what is pure delight—
> Not all that pleases is substantial good;
> Not all which grieves, true ill, well understood—
> That, of all joys, must be pronounced the best,
> Which virtue's arduous triumphs yield the breast.

In this story may be perceived the germs both of Fletcher's *Faithful Shepherdess* and of Luzzatto's *Unto the Upright Praise*. But while the former seized upon and elaborated the sensuous element in Guarini's plot, giving us a truly disgusting figure

127

in Chloe, Luzzatto pounced on the finer aspects, and his heroines outshine even Amarillis in purity and beauty of mind, just as his heroes surpass Mirtillo in fidelity to the standards of manhood. That one and the same model should have produced two such varied copies says much for the genius of the original author. To him, it is true, we owe the tragi-comedy of intrigue. But to him also we are indebted for idylls, as full-blooded as those of Theocritus, but far more spiritual.

HAHN'S NOTE BOOK

The Hahn family came to Frankfort-on-the-Main from Nordlingen (Bavaria), whence the Jews were expelled in 1507. Between that date and 1860 Nordlingen could not boast of a synagogue; such Jews as visited the place were admitted for a day at a time to the fairs, or were allowed temporarily to reside in war times. In each case a poll-tax was exacted (see *Jewish Encyclopedia,* vol. ix, p. 335). In Frankfort, the family dwelt in a house bearing the sign of " The Red Cock " (*Zum rothen Hahn*). Graetz fully describes the regulations which compelled the Jews of Frankfort to fix shields with various devices and names on their houses. He cites " the garlic," " the ass," " green shield," " red shield " (Rothschild), " dragon." The Frankfort Jews were forced to name themselves after these shields. Hence, in the Jewish sources, the author with whom we are now concerned is sometimes called Joseph Nordlinger, from his original home, and sometimes Joseph Hahn, from the family house-sign in Frankfort.

He himself was not permitted to live peaceably in Frankfort. Born in the second half of the sixteenth century, he not only had to endure the pitiable restrictions to which the Jews were at normal times subjected, but he suffered in 1614 under the Fettmilch riot, as the result of which, after many of the whole Jewish community had been slain and more injured, the survivors left the town. In March, 1616, the Jews—Joseph Hahn among them—were welcomed back amid public demonstrations of good-will, and the community instituted the Frankfort Purim on Adar 20, the anniversary of the return. Though the trouble thus ended happily, we can understand how insecure the life of the German Jews was at the beginning of the seventeenth century. Hence we need not be surprised to find in Hahn's book *Yosif Omez* (§ 483) a form of dying confession drawn up in Frankfort to be recited by those undergoing martyrdom. It is a moving composition, simple in its pathos, yet too poignant in its note of sorrow to be cited here in full.

Let it not be thought, however, that the book is a doleful one. Joseph Hahn's is a warm-hearted Judaism, and there was room in it for a manifold human interest. The work, in a sense, is learned, but it is written so crisply and epigrammatically that its charm surpasses and even disguises its technicalities. It was printed in 1723, but was written a good deal earlier, as we know that the author died in 1637. I have alluded to the manifold interests which occupied Hahn's mind. Questions of Jewish law and fundamental problems of morality are considered; but so are matters of costume and cookery. How to wear a special dress for synagogue and how to keep a special overcoat for the benediction of the moon, how to rub off ink-stains from the fingers before meals, how " it is a truer penance to eat moderately at ordinary meals than to endure an occasional fast," how the children should be encouraged to read good books at table, and how, when such a book is finished, there should be a jolly *siyyum*—these and many another interesting view crowd Joseph Hahn's delightful pages. He enjoyed a cheerful meal, but he proceeds to denounce in unmeasured terms those who (" and there are many such in our times," he adds) sing love-songs or tell indecent stories over their wine. " Do not esteem lightly," he cautions his readers (§ 183), " the advice of our sages," as to first putting on the right shoe and first removing the left. Joseph Hahn, in truth, is a remarkable mixture of the old and the new; he loves old customs, yet constantly praises new ones, such as the introduction of Psalms and of *Lekah Dodi* into the Friday night service. We are so familiar with the hymn " Come, O friend, to meet the bride," that it is startling to be reminded that it dates from the sixteenth century. Joseph Hahn thoroughly entered into the spirit of such lively processions from place to place as accompanied *Lekah Dodi,* though he held them more suitable for Palestine than Germany. He detested low songs, and objected to games of chance, but he was no kill-joy. Again and again he refers to the synagogue tunes, and revels in *hazzanut.* His was a thoroughly Jewish synthesis of austerity and joviality.

He has many remarks as to the proper treatment of servants. An employer shall not retain wages in trust for the servant, even at the latter's desire. He must first pay the wages, and the servant may then ask the employer to save it (§ 361). He had a very loving heart as well as a just mind. Delightful is his custom of saying *Sheheheyanu* on seeing a friend or beloved relative after an interval of thirty days. On the other hand, he, with equal gravity, tells us (§ 455) how his father,

when he left the city, took a little splinter of wood
from the gate, and fixed it in his hat-band, as a
specific for his safety, or sure return. This is a
wide-spread custom. The whole book is a wonderful union of sound sense and quaintness. The
author, in the midst of deep ritual problems and of
careful philological discussions of liturgical points,
will turn aside to warn us against buying the Sabbath fish on Thursday. Fish, he says, must be
fresh. In the same breath he has this fine remark:
" What you eat profits the body; what you spare
for God (that is, give to the poor) profits the
soul." He protests (§ 547) against permitting the
poor to go round to beg from house to house;
officials must be appointed to carry relief to the
needy in their homes. But do not forget to taste
your *shalet* on Friday to test whether it be properly
cooked! One of the most characteristically Jewish features of life under the traditional *régime*
was the *man's* participation in the kitchen prepara-
tions. But Joseph Hahn takes a high view of the
woman's part in the moralization of the domestic
life. Just as the husband was not excluded from
the kitchen, so the wife was not limited to it. Yet
Hahn would not allow women to sing the *Zemirot*
or table hymns.

I have said that our author loves the old, yet has
no objection to the new. The latter feature is ex-
emplified by a long song on the Sabbath Light, composed by Joseph Hahn for Friday nights. Each
verse is printed in Hebrew (§ 601) with a Yiddish
paraphrase. He disliked setting the *Zemirot* to
non-Jewish tunes. There is no sense, he adds, in
the argument of those who urge that these non-
Jewish tunes were stolen from the temple melodies! The children, we learn, had a special Sabbath
cake. A Jewish child, he relates (§ 612), was
carried off by robbers, but cried so pitifully for his
cake on Friday night, that he was eventually discovered by Jews and ransomed. He protests
against the " modern innovation " of introducing
a sermon in the morning service; this compels the
old and ailing to wait too long for breakfast. The
sermon must, as of old, be given after the meal
(§ 625). Yet he did not mind himself introducing
an innovation, for he instituted a simple haggadic
discourse on the afternoons of festivals, so as to
attract the people and keep them from frivolous
amusements (§ 821). The greater *Spinholz* on
the Saturday before a wedding was still customary
in the author's time. He complains of those people
who drink better wine on Sundays than on Satur-

days (§ 693). He objects to the practice of the rich to have their daughters taught instrumental music by male instructors (§ 890). But here I must break off, though it is difficult to tear oneself from the book, even the narrowness of which has a historical interest, and the prejudices of which entertain. As a whole, it represents a phase of Jewish life which belongs to the past, yet there runs through it a vein of homely sentiment which is found also in our present.

LEON MODENA'S " RITES "

Said to have been composed at the request of an English nobleman for the delectation of James I, Leon Modena's account of Jewish ceremonial was certainly intended for Christian readers. Though written in Italian, it first appeared in France (Paris, 1637), through the good offices of the author's pupil and friend, J. Gaffarel. It was the source of a whole library of similar books. Not only was it translated into several languages, but onwards from Modena's time, writers, Jewish and Christian, competent and incompetent, devoted themselves to the task of presenting to the world in general the teachings and customs of Judaism. The recent treatise of Oesterley and Box is a lineal descendant of Modena's *Rites*.

Of the author it may be said that he was the Admirable Crichton of his age (1571-1648). His range of knowledge and power was extraordinary. As Dr. Johnson said of Oliver Goldsmith, he touched nothing which he did not adorn. Besides writing many books on many subjects, he filled the office of Rabbi at Venice with distinction, his sermons in Italian attracting large audiences. Some of his German critics call him " characterless." Why? Because he denounced gambling, and yet was a life-long victim to the vice. In his boyhood he produced a pamphlet against card-playing, and in 1631 successfully protested against the excommunication of card-players. But is there lack of character here? Of many another great man could it be said that he saw and approved the better yet followed the worse. And there are things which one dislikes without wishing to put the offenders under a ban. On another occasion, Modena severely attacked Rabbinism, and then published a reply to his own attack. He assuredly was not the only man impelled to refute his own arguments.

Modena was, one might rather say, a man of moods, and therefore of singular openness and width of mind. He suffered not from lack of character, but from an excess of impressionability. A bee has not less character than a caterpillar, because the former flies from flower to flower, while the latter adheres to the same cabbage leaf. Modena, to put the case in yet another way, lived at a transitional period, when Jews were only beginning to acclimatize themselves to modern conditions, and when settled views on many subjects were not only

137

difficult but undesirable. Despite his vagaries, one is rather attracted to him. There must have been solidity as well as versatility in his disposition, or he could not possibly have retained the important rabbinic post he filled for more than half-a-century. Probably the secret was that he not only possessed personal charm, but the real man was best known to those who knew him best. They—or many of them—assuredly admired and loved him.

We will now turn to another figure—the first English translator of Modena's *Riti Ebraici*. This was Edmund Chilmead, who was born in 1610 and died in 1654. He was a good scholar and an accomplished musician. Up to 1648 he resided in Oxford, but as a result of the troubles between Charles I and the Parliament, he was expelled from the University because of his royalist opinions. Two things, however, speak well for Cromwell's toleration. Chilmead was not only allowed to live unmolested in London to the day of his death, but had no hesitation, on the title-page of his translation of Modena, to describe himself still as " Chaplain of Christ Church, Oxon." The date of the translation gives the clue. " The History of the Rites, Customes, and Manner of Life of the Present Jews throughout the World " was printed " for

Jo. Martin and Jo. Ridley, at the Castle in Fleet Street, by Ram Alley " in 1650. By that time Cromwell was probably thinking of the Jewish question, and he must have welcomed this first-hand statement on the Jewish religion. Chilmead's edition, one must confess, is badly printed, and is not very creditable to the printing capacity of the " Castle in Fleet Street." One might pardon the many misprints in the Hebrew, but it is hard to overlook the numerous faults in the English. It is not wonderful that, in the following century, Ockley thought it necessary to issue a new version.

Modena's own original was not, as the title suggests, a history. It does not so much give sources as facts. But this circumstance, that it is mainly *descriptive,* confers on it a permanent value. For it thus becomes a document. It helps us to realize several aspects of the Jewish position at the beginning of the seventeenth century. The author uses the term *history* in the sense of narrative; as he states in his Prefatory Epistle, he is concerned with the *what* and not with the *why* (" Quod sunt," not " Propter quod sunt," as he expresses it). He deals with his present, not with the past, and for that very limitation we may be grateful. He claims, too, that he is a " Relater," not a " De-

fender." That being so, it is of peculiar interest
to find what we do in his work, arranged in five
books, " according to the number of the Books of
the Law."

Several forms of prayer appear for the first time
in his pages. Certainly Chilmead is the earliest to
give us in English the Prayer for the Government,
or a translation of the Thirteen Articles drawn up
by Maimonides. Modena, again, tells us that in
his day it was customary to " leave about a yard
square of the wall of the house unplaistered on
which they write either the verse of Psalm 137, ' If
I forget thee, O Jerusalem,' or the words *Zecher
Lahorban*—a Memorial of the Desolation." He
knows only *wooden* Mezuzahs. Jews in Italy have
pictures and images in their houses, " especially if
they be not with Relief, or Imbossed work, nor the
Bodies at large." Few, he reports, take heed to
the custom of placing the beds north and south;
many attach significance to dreams. Jewish men
never paint their faces, for the custom is " effemi-
nate "; and " in whatsoever country they are, they
(the men) usually affect the long garment, or
Gown." The women dress " in the habite of the
countries where they inhabite "; but after marriage
wear a *perruke* to cover their natural hair. The

Jews build their synagogues wherever they can, " it being impossible for them now to erect any statelie or sumptuous Fabricks." Things, as we know, soon after Modena's time became different, for by the middle of the seventeenth century, several fine synagogues were built in Rome and elsewhere. The women " see whatever is done in the *School* (thus Chilmead renders *scuola* or synagogue), though they are themselves unseen of any man." In the same city there will be places of worship " according to the different customes of the Levantines, Dutch (German), and Italians." Then, " in their singing, the Dutch far exceed all the rest: the Levantines and Spaniards use a certain singing tone, much after the Turkish manner; and the Italians affect a more plain, and quiet way in their devotions." The " Favours " of " having a hand " in the acts connected with the reading of the Law " are bought of the Chaunter, and he that biddeth most, shall have a share in them."

Willingly, did space permit, we would follow the author through his account of the Judaism of his time. The majority of Jews, he says, are poor, yet annually they send " Almes to Jerusalem, Safed, Tiberias, and Hebron." The Jews never " torment, or abuse, or put to any cruel death, any Brute

141

Beast." Very few Jews are able to speak Hebrew; all learn the language of the countries where they are born. " Onely those of the Morea still retain the Hebrew Tongue also, and use it in their Familiar Letters." In Italy, he records, the Talmud " continues utterly prohibited," and copies are not to be found in the country. Jews do not regard " Vowes " as " commendable "; yet " when they are made, they ought to be kept." Not many now observe the " tradition " against eating " Fish and Flesh together." He tells us of an arrangement by which, for the Sabbath, some " so ordered the matter aforehand, that the Fire should kindle itself at such and such a time." The Passover bread is made in " flat cakes of divers forms and shapes." The " Ceremonie with a Cock," on the eve of the Day of Atonement, " is now left off both in the East and in Italy, as being a thing both Superstitious and Groundlesse." But they still, on Purim, " as often as they hear Haman named, beat the ground, and make a great murmuring noise." Bigamy " is seldome or never used." Marriages are usually performed before full moon, and the favorite days are Wednesdays and Fridays, with Thursdays for widows. " Little boyes, with lighted torches in their hands," sing before the bridal couple, who are seated under the canopy. The Ketubah is read at the marriage. Modena mentions the charms against *Lilit,* and name-changing in case of sickness. He describes how, in Germany, in the case of girls, " the Chaunter goeth home to the Parents house, and lifting the child's cradle on high, he blesseth it, and so giveth it the Name." Modena also informs us that the Karaites were, in his time, numerous in Constantinople, Cairo, and Russia.

Modena records that among the Jews " there are many women that are much more devout and pious than the men, and who not only endeavour to bring up their children in all manner of Vertuous Education; but are a means also of restraining their husbands from their Vitious Courses, they would otherwise take, and of inclining them to a more Godly way of Life." With which handsome and just compliment we will take leave of our author.

PART III

Part III

MENASSEH AND REMBRANDT

On April 25, 1655, six months before starting on his mission to Cromwell, Menasseh ben Israel—visionary about to play the rôle of statesman—completed in Amsterdam the Spanish book which forms the subject of this paper. Duodecimo in size (5¼ x 2⅞ inches), it consists of 12 + 259 pages, with a list of the author's works published or projected, and on the last of the unpaginated leaves a Latin version of Psalm 126. In the catalogue of his works appended to the *Vindiciæ Judæorum* (London, 1656) Menasseh includes "*Piedra pretiosa,* of *Nebuchadnezzar's* image, or the fifth Monarchy." This was not, however, the real title. The title was, in truth, in Hebrew *Eben Yekarah,* and in Spanish *Piedra Gloriosa,* i. e., the "Precious Stone." The date given above for the completion of the book is fixed by the dedication, which is addressed to Menasseh's Christian friend, Isaac Vossius.

147

On a casual glance the book seems a hopeless jumble of incongruities. Nebuchadnezzar's image, Jacob's dream, the combat of David and Goliath, the vision of Ezekiel—what have these in common, and what has the title to do with them? The answer to these questions is soon found.

The whole work is Messianic, and in his usual symbolic style, Menasseh seizes on a " Stone " as the central feature for his little treatise. There was the stone, " cut out without hands," which smote the image seen by the king of Babylon. There was the stone, gathered from the field of Beth-el, on which Jacob laid his weary head to rest when fleeing from his brother. There was the stone, picked smooth from the brook, with which David slew the Philistine. Perhaps the three were one and the same stone, Menasseh seems to imply. Anyhow, he saw in all these incidents a Messianic reference. Nebuchadnezzar's image, with its feet of clay, typified the Gentiles that were to rise and fall before the great day of the Lord. The ladder of Jacob, with its ascending and descending angels, typified again the rise and fall of nations. David's victory over Goliath foreshadowed the triumph of the Messiah over the powers of earth. And the whole is rounded off with Ezekiel's vision of the

MENASSEH BEN ISRAEL
(From an etching by Rembrandt, in the possession of
Mr. Felix Warburg, New York)

chariot with its strange beasts and emblems—a chariot which, in the view accepted by Menasseh, typified the Kingdom of the Messiah.

Following the dedication to Vossius is an explanatory note to " the Reader." In this note the author explains that to make his meaning clear he has added four illustrations. He does not name the artist. But we know that he was none other than Menasseh's neighbor and intimate, Rembrandt. Four etchings, signed by Rembrandt and dated 1654, are possessed by more than one library; probably the fullest sets are to be found in the Fitzwilliam and British Museums. They were originally etched on one plate, which was afterwards cut into four. When all four etchings formed one plate, the arrangement was (as Mr. Middleton explains in his *Descriptive Catalogue of the Etched Work of Rembrandt*, p. 240) :

(I) Upper left: *Nebuchadnezzar's Image.* Clothed only about the loins; there is a band or fillet about the head, and a short cloak hangs behind. The stone which breaks the legs of the image (the feet are seen falling to the left) has been cast from a roughly shaped rock. The stone is near part of a globe; illustrating the text " And the stone that broke the image became a great mountain, *and filled the whole earth*"(Daniel

2. 35). The brow is inscribed "Babel," the right and left arms "Persae" and "Medi," the waist "Graeci," the legs "Romani" and "Mahometani." These names only appear in the *fifth* "state" of the etching. There's a proof of the fourth "state" in Paris, which bears the names written in Rembrandt's own hand.

(II) Upper right: *Vision of Ezekiel*. The lower part, in the foreground, shows the four creatures of the chariot; above is a "glory," amid the rays of which is seen the Almighty, surrounded by adoring angels.

(III) Lower left: *Jacob's Ladder*. The patriarch, bearded, lies half-way up the ladder, tended by an angel, others are bending down in gaze, while one figure is seen mounting the rungs immediately above.

(IV) Lower right: *Combat of David and Goliath*. The most spirited drawing of all; in a scene overhung by rocks with warriors looking on, the giant grasps his lance in his left hand and with shield advanced on his right arm is charging David, who has his sling in action over his right shoulder.

The Museum, as already implied, possesses proof of the etchings in various "states"—the artist touched and retouched them, until they assumed the state reproduced by the present writer in 1906, in commemoration of the tercentenary of Rembrandt's birth. The etchings are beautiful tokens of sympathy between the Rabbi and the painter. The various "states" show, as Mr. I. Solomons has suggested, that Rembrandt took unremitting pains to obtain Menasseh's approval of his work.

Yet he failed to win this approval. It is pretty certain that the etchings were never used. Mr. Fairfax Murray possessed the *Piedra Gloriosa* with the etchings, and has now presented the volume to the University Library, Cambridge; another copy is to be seen in the Musée Carnavalet, Paris, a copy formerly owned by M. Dutuit of Rouen. But Mr. Solomons seems right in asserting that " the original etchings in the copies of Mr. Murray and M. Dutuit were no doubt inserted after by admirers of Rembrandt's work, but certainly not with the knowledge and sanction of Menasseh." Why not? The etchings are good work; they really illustrate their subject, and must have added to the commercial, as well as to the artistic value of Menasseh's work.

The most curious fact is that, though Rembrandt's etchings were never used, a set of copperplate engravings, based, as Mr. Solomons guesses, by the Jewish engraver Salom Italia on Rembrandt but not identical with his work, is found in some copies of Menasseh's book—copies possessed by Mr. Solomons, M. Didot, and the Levy Collection in Hamburg. These engravings are laterally inverted, the right of Rembrandt's etchings becomes the left of Salom Italia's engravings. There are other differences in detail, all calculated to render the pictures more fitted for book illustration, but of all the changes only one is of consequence, and it was Mr. Solomons who detected the real significance of the change.

The change referred to gives the clue to the whole mystery. On comparing the two versions of the Vision of Ezekiel a striking variation is discernible. The figure of the Almighty has been suppressed! Here was the fatal defect in Rembrandt's work. Menasseh could not possibly use a drawing in which the Deity is represented; he was not the one to repeat the inadvertence of the artist of the Sarajevo Haggadah. Possibly he only detected the fault at the last hour. But a fatality clung to the second set of illustrations also. Several copies of the *Piedra Gloriosa* are extant without any pictures at all.

LANCELOT ADDISON ON THE BARBARY JEWS

" Justice is done to the private virtues of the Jews of Barbary." So Mr. Francis Espinasse remarks in his biography of Lancelot Addison. It is an accurate comment. Lancelot, the father of the more famous Joseph Addison—who himself wrote so amiably of the Jews a generation later—spent several years in Africa as English chaplain. Born in 1632, he showed an independent mind at Oxford. He roughly handled some of the University Puritans in 1658, and was promptly compelled to recant his speech on his knees in open Convocation. Tangier came into the possession of Charles II in 1662. Lancelot Addison had officiated in Dunkirk for the previous three years; but when that port was given up to the French, Addison was transferred to Morocco.

Here he kept his eyes open. Several lively volumes came from him on Tangier life, on Mohammedanism, on Moorish politics. The most remarkable of these deals with the Jews. So popular was this volume on their " Present State " that three editions were called for. The first came out in 1675. If one may judge by the British Museum copy, it lacked the awesome frontispiece which may be seen in the edition of 1676. Though superscribed "The Present State of the Jews in Barbary," the almost naked figure is not meant to represent a' child of Israel. The personage depicted wears a gorgeously feathered hat and a short waist-covering, also of feathers. Add to this a spear bigger than its wielder, and you have his full costume. It is less Addison's than his illustrator's idea of a typical Moor.

From the very opening paragraph of the dedication we see that Lancelot possessed some of his son's gift of gentle humor. He had inscribed a former book to Secretary Williamson, and he now repeats the act, " it faring with Scriblers, as with those Votaries who never forsake the Saint they once finde propitious." As for his account of the Jews, he claims that his is more " particular and true " than other descriptions, " this being," he says, " the result of Conversation and not of Report." (" Conversation," of course, he uses in the old sense of " direct intercourse "). Some of the modern assailants of the Jews who appropriate aristocratic names will hardly like Addison's justification of his interest. It is because of their clear genealogies and ancient lineage that he in the first instance admires the Jews. And if their ancestry was noble, they were not less happy in their primitive religion. " Now seeing that they have been the channel of so many benefits to the rest of mankind, they ought to be the matter of our thankful Reflection, and not of our obloquy and reproach."

With fine indignation, he goes on to resent the manner in which the Jews of Barbary were " lorded over by the imperious and haughty Moor." The Moorish boys beat the Jewish children, and the latter dare not retaliate. " The Moors permit not the Jews the possession of any war-like weapons, unless in point of Trade." Addison adds that this gratifies the Jews, who are, he asserts, as " destitute of true courage as of good nature." It is important to remember these severe remarks on the Jewish character, as it shows that when the author praises he does so not from partiality but from conviction. Curiously enough, he has hardly done calling them cowards, when he tells us that the Christians and Moors use the Jews for " sending them upon hazardous messages," such as " collecting the maritime imposts," an office which must have needed more than a little hardihood.

Our author contrasts the black caps of the Jews with the red of the Moors, and has other quaint details as to costume. He then calls attention to the religious unanimity of the Jews. " They are signally vigilant to avoid divisions, as looking upon those among Christian Professors, to be an argument against the truth of the things they profess." This is amusing, coming from a man who, throughout his life, was a rather sturdy opponent of union among the Christian bodies. And what would he think of the unity among Jews if he could see *our* " present state "? Addison then enters into a eulogy of the sobriety and temperance of the Jews; he terms their conduct " well civilised," and declares that they " cannot be charged with any of those Debauches which are grown unto reputation with whole nations of Christians." Then he specifies. " Adultery, Drunkenness, Gluttony, Pride of Apparel, etc., are so far from being in request with them that they are scandalised at their frequent practice in Christians." Again and again the author laments that he has to praise the Synagogue at the expense of the Church. But he takes it out in firm abuse of the rabbinic theology, information on which he obtained from a local Rabbi, " Aaron Ben-Netas "—a not unlearned man, he says, one who only needed to be a Christian to be thoroughly worthy of esteem.

But we must pass over Addison's elaborate analysis of the Jewish creed, and of his many curious and mostly accurate details on rites and superstitions. The notable thing is that as soon as he touches fundamental social questions, his eulogy of the Jews reappears. " Orderly and decent " are the adjectives he uses of the Jewish marriage customs. I regret that I am unable to find space for Addison's allusion to the fashions of dressing the brides for the canopies, or rather " bowers and arbours," which in Barbary replaced the canopies used in other countries. Thus the custom in some American homes of performing Jewish marriages under a floral bower rather than a canopy has its analogue in the past. Very significant is another statement about marriage. Theoretically he found polygamy defended, but monogamy was the rule of life. " The Jews of whom I now write, though they greatly magnify and extol the concession of polygamy, yet they are not very fond of its practice." He ascribes this abstinence to policy rather than to religion, and there is more truth in this than Addison saw. For such social institutions are entirely a matter for the social conscience, and "policy" dictates them. So long as social institutions remain within the bounds of such sanctification as religion can approve, religion must be content to follow "policy." Monogamy is so clearly felt to be the best policy for mankind, under modern conditions, that religion in the West maintains it. "Religion" and "policy" are here at one.

Addison fairly gives his enthusiasm the rein when he discusses Jewish education. "The care of the Jews is very laudable in this particular, there being not many people in the world more watchful to have their children early tinctured with religion than the present Hebrews." Though they usually speak "*Moresco,* the Language of their Nativity, and a sort of Spanish which enables them for Traffick," they learn Hebrew. The children, he informs us, are usually taught the Hebrew for the domestic utensils and "terms of Traffick Negotiation." The method was quite in accord with modern ideas of teaching a language. "By this Order they furnish the Children with a *Nomenclature of Hebrew* Words; and all this before they admit them to Syntax and Construction." Addison pictures the Jewish Sabbath with some charm; he even cites passages from Luria, to whom the home

158

and synagogue rites of the day of rest owe so much. On no subject is our author more interesting than with regard to the Jewish charities. The Jews live " in a more mutual charity of alms than either the Moor or Christians "; and Addison admits, " it cannot be denied that the Jews' manner of relieving the poor, is regular and commendable." In his day it was, as it is in ours, the Synagogue's ideal to relieve its own poor. There were no beggars in the Barbary Jewry. " For though among the Jews of Barbary there is a great store of needy persons, yet they are supplied after a manner which much conceals (as to men of other religions) their poverty." Obviously Addison would like these people to become Christians. Why do they refuse? The " stiffness of their necks," on the one hand, and the " naughtiness of our lives," on the other, cries the author. The " naughtiness " will, let us hope, be more easily removed than the " stiffness." Lancelot Addison, says Macaulay, " made some figure in the world." He deserved to do so. His book on the Jews was a credit to his power of observation and his goodness of heart.

THE BODENSCHATZ PICTURES

Johann Christoph Georg Bodenschatz, a priest of Uttenreuth, underwent a triple training for his great work on Jewish Ceremonial. He studied literature, observed facts, and used his hands. The *Jewish Encyclopedia* remarks that he "is said to have made elaborate models of the Ark of Noah and of the Tabernacle in the Wilderness." There is no reason for the qualifying words "is said." In a dedicatory epistle to the Margrave Friederich of Brandenburg, Bodenschatz distinctly informs us that in 1739 he constructed these models, "after the records of Scripture and of Jewish Antiquities." He adds that the models were preserved in the royal *Kunst und Naturaliencabinet*. I cannot say whether they still exist; but at the beginning of last century, the Tabernacle was at Bayreuth and the Ark at Nuremberg.

In 1748 Bodenschatz began to issue his work on the Jews; he completed the publication in the next year. In it he dealt with the Jewish religion (*Kirchliche Verfassung der heutigen Juden, sonderlich derer in Deutschland*). He had planned a continuation on the Civil Laws of the Synagogue. But he left it unfinished, though he lived another half-century. Perhaps he had exhausted all his means, for the thirty copper-plates must have been expensive. The very title-page states he paid for them out of his own pocket. These illustrations he introduced with a double object: they were, in part, to serve as an ornament, but chiefly as an elucidation of the text. Both his book and his pictures became very popular, and did much to secure for Judaism a favorable consideration in Germany.

As we know that Bodenschatz possessed some artistic skill, we may safely assume that he inspired and assisted the artists whom he employed. He does not appear, however, to have done any of the drawings with his own hand. Nearly all the pictures are signed. Most of them were designed by Eichler in Erlangen, and engraved by G. Nusbiegel in Nuremberg. Both of these belonged to artistic families; there were three generations of Eichlers, and a Nusbiegel engraved illustrations for Lavater's works. One of the Bodenschatz pictures was engraved by C. M. Roth; another, among the best of the whole series—the illustration of Shehitah—was drawn by Johann Conrad Müller. It would be interesting to collect the names of those Christian artists and mechanics who, in the seventeenth and eighteenth centuries, were engaged in illustrating books on Judaism. There was, for instance, the Englishman R. Vaughan who worked at Josephus (Josippon) ; there was the Frenchman Bernard Picart; and there were very many others, though the exquisite medallions, which adorn the title-pages of all six volumes of Surrenhusius' Latin Mishnah, were from a Jewish hand.

Bodenschatz made use of his predecessor Picart, whose twenty plates illustrative of the " Ceremonies des Juifs " appeared in Amsterdam in 1723. But what he chiefly owed to Picart was the composition of the groups; the details are mostly original. Similarly he derived his idea for the processions of the bride and the bridegroom, with their musical performers, from Kirchner, but here, again, the details are his own, and the total effect is full of charm. I do not wish, by any means, to depreciate Kirchner, who in his *Jüdisches Ceremoniel* (1726) has some fine engravings. One of them, depicting the preparation of the Passover bread, is as vigorous as anything in Bodenschatz, though I think that the latter is, on the average, superior to Kirchner. Readers can easily judge the character both of the Bodenschatz and the Kirchner pictures from the specimens so wisely reproduced in the volumes of the *Jewish Encyclopedia*. No one need complain that the *Encyclopedia* prints these illustrations too profusely. For—to limit my remarks to Bodenschatz—though copies of that worthy's book are common enough, many of them are incomplete. From the British Museum example, six of the thirty plates are missing; the Cambridge copy also lacks some of the plates, in particular the marriage ceremony under the canopy, which, however, may be seen in the *Jewish Encyclopedia*, vol. vi, p. 504. On the other hand, the *Encyclopedia* (vol. iii, p. 432) somewhat exaggerates the glare of the eyes in the grim realism of Bodenschatz's picture of an interment.

What is assuredly one of the most interesting of Bodenschatz's plates does not, so far as I have noticed, appear in the *Encyclopedia*. I refer to the Pentecost celebrations, where Bodenschatz shows us both the cut flowers and the growing plants in the synagogue decorations of the day. The floral border of this plate is particularly well conceived. Very attractive, too, is the picture of Blessing the New Moon: the outlines of the houses stand out in bold relief. Bodenschatz is careful to inform us that the favorite time for the ceremony is a

Saturday night, when the men are still dressed in their Sabbath clothes, and thus make a good show. The Priestly Benediction is also a notable success; the Cohen with his hands to his eyes impresses. More than once Bodenschatz depicts a curious scene, once common now almost unknown. On the front of the synagogue is a star, cut in stone, and after the marriage the husband shatters a vessel by casting it at the star. The glass, where the custom is retained, is now broken under the canopy. By the way, the author also introduces us to the more familiar ceremony of the same nature at the actual wedding or betrothal. Altogether ingenious is the plate on which are diagrammatically represented the various forms of boundaries connected with the Sabbath law.

Naturally a goodly number of the pictures deal with curiosities. The quainter side of Jewish ceremonial obviously appeals to an artist. Thus the waving of the cock before the Day of Atonement, the *Lilit* inscriptions over the bed of the new-born infant, the Mikweh, the Halizah shoe, make their due appearance. But Bodenschatz does not show these things to ridicule them. He is among the most objective of those who, before our own days, sought to reproduce synagogue scenes. He must have had a very full experience of these scenes; he must have been an eye-witness. It would seem as though he meant us to gather this from one of his Sabbath pictures, of which he has several. I do not refer to the vividness of the touches in his representation of the Friday night at home—though this illustration presupposes personal knowledge. Nor do I refer to his pictures of Sabbath ovens, for these could have been examined in shops. But what I allude to is this. In his picture of the interior of the synagogue, we see the Sabbath service in progress. Standing on the right, looking on, is a hatless observer. Does Bodenschatz mean this for himself, thus suggesting that he had often been a spectator where the rest were participators? It may be so. Anyhow, most of those who have had to steep themselves in literature of this kind have a warm feeling of regard for Bodenschatz. He was not invariably just, but he was never unkind; no mistakes that he made (and he is on the whole conspicuously accurate) were due to prejudice. Any scholar, any artist, would be proud to deserve such a verdict.

LESSING'S FIRST JEWISH PLAY

There are bigger virtues than consistency, and I
have spared a good word for that human chame-
leon Leon Modena. But, undeniably, a great
career is all the nobler when through it there runs
a consistent purpose. Wordsworth, in a famous
poem, asked:

> Who is the happy warrior? Who is he
> That every man in arms should wish to be?

And the first sentence of his answer runs:

> It is the generous spirit, who, when brought
> Among the tasks of real life, hath wrought
> Upon the plan that pleased his childish thought.

If this be so, then Lessing was a happy warrior
indeed. For religious tolerance is interwoven with
his combative life. It was the ideal of his boyhood
and of his age. It is to be seen in his " Nathan,"
the masterpiece of his mature genius, and it equally
underlay his youthful drama *The Jews*. Nathan
the Wise is Mendelssohn, and was drawn on the
basis of experience; but the " Traveller," who is the
hero of *Die Juden* is no individual, having been
drawn by Lessing out of his own good heart.
Thirty years separate the two plays (written, re-

spectively, in 1749 and 1779). But they are united in spirit.

Die Juden is a short composition, even though it includes twenty-three scenes. Some of these scenes are very brief. The plot is quite simple. A baron and his daughter are saved by a traveller from robbers; the impression made by the rescuer is so great, that the baron is inclined to find in him a son-in-law. Then the traveller reveals the fact that he is a Jew. Baron and Jew part with mutual esteem. Dramatically, the play is not of much merit. The " Traveller " is not so much a person as a personification. He is the type of virtue, honor, magnanimity. He leaves one cold, not because, as Michaelis objected in 1754, he is impossibly, or at least improbably, perfect, but because he is crudely and mechanically drawn. Mendelssohn completely rebutted the criticism of Michaelis; but, none the less, the " Traveller " possesses little of that human, personal quality which makes " Nathan " so convincing and interesting. On the other hand, the baron is admirably painted. He is not a bigoted Jew-hater; he is simply animated by a conventional dislike of Jews. Lessing, even in his student years, was too good an artist to daub on his colors too glaringly.

The importance of *Die Juden* is to be found, as we have seen, in its anticipation of *Nathan der Weise*. Sometimes the identity of thought is strikingly close. In the fourth act of *Nathan* occurs this dialogue:

Friar: Nathan! Nathan! You are a Christian! By God, you are a Christian! There never was a better Christian!

Nathan: We are of one mind! For that which makes me, in your eyes, a Christian, makes you, in my eyes, a Jew!

Compare (as Niemeyer has done) the exchanges in *Die Juden:*

Baron: How estimable would the Jews be if they were all like you!

Traveller: And how admirable the Christians, if they all possessed your qualities!

A Tsar is said to have repeated pretty much the baron's speech to Sir Moses Montefiore. It is not recorded that the latter made the traveller's reply.

Edmund Burke, in one of his speeches on America, protested that it was impossible to draw up " an indictment against a whole people." He forgot the frequency with which such indictments are drawn up against the Jews. Now if there was one thing that more than the rest roused Lessing's anger, it was just this tarring of all Jews with one brush. One can conceive the glee with which Lessing wrote the passage in which the baron commits this very offence, unconscious of his peculiarly unfortunate *faux pas*, for he has no notion yet that the traveller is a Jew:

Baron: It seems to me that the very faces of the Jews prejudice one against them. You can read in their eyes their maliciousness, deceit, perjury. Why do you turn away from me?

Traveller: I see you are very learned in physiognomies—I am afraid, sir, that mine . . . .

Baron: O, you wrong me! How could you entertain such a suspicion? Without being learned in physiognomies, I must tell you I have never met with a more frank, generous, and pleasing countenance than yours.

Traveller: To tell you the truth, I do not approve of generalizations concerning a whole people . . . . I should think that among all nations good and wicked are to be found.

These quotations will suffice to convey an idea of the aim of the dramatist and of the manner in which it is carried out. There is a certain amount of comic relief to the gravity of the main plot. The foot-pad and garroter, Martin Krumm, cuts an amusing figure as an assailant of the honesty of the Jews. "A Christian would have given me a kick in the ribs and not a snuff-box," says Christopher, the traveller's servant. Christopher is a funny rogue. When his master cannot find him, and naturally complains, the servant replies: " I can only be in one place at one time. Is it my fault that you did not go to that place? You say you

169

have to search for me? Surely you'll always find me where I am."

There were a few attempts prior to Lessing to present the Jew in a favorable light on the stage, as Sir Sidney Lee has shown. But between Shylock and Nathan there stretches a lurid desert, broken only by the oasis of *Die Juden*. To some it may occur that the battle of tolerance fought by Lessing did not end in a permanent victory. Lessing himself would not have been disquieted at that result. As he expressed it, the search for truth rather than the possession of truth is the highest human good. A leading Viennese paper said some few years ago that if *Nathan the Wise* had been written now, it would have been hissed off the German stage. It is not unlikely. Fortunately, Lessing wrote before 1880! *Nathan* does not remain unacted. I saw Possart play the title-role in Munich in the nineties. His splendid elocution carried off Nathan's long speeches with wonderful absence of monotony.

A thing of truth is a boon forever, because it makes further progress in truth-seeking certain. Because there has been one Lessing, there *must* be others. And if *Nathan the Wise* be thus a lasting inspiration, let us not forget that the poet was trying his hand, and maturing his powers, by writing the play which has served as the subject of this sketch.   170

ISAAC PINTO'S PRAYER-BOOK

It was in America that the first English translation of the Synagogue Prayer-Book appeared (1761 and 1766). Often has attention been drawn to the curiosity that this latter volume was published not in London but in New York. The 1761 edition has only recently been discovered by Dr. Pool; with the 1766 work we have long been familiar. According to the *Bibliotheca Anglo-Judaica* (p. 174), " the Mahamad would not allow a translation to be printed in England." If such a refusal was made, we must at least amend the last words, and read *in English* for *in England*. For it was in London, in 1740, that Isaac Nieto's *Spanish* rendering of the prayers for New Year and Day of Atonement saw the light of publication.

Indeed, in Isaac Pinto's preface the point is made quite clear. " In Europe," he says, " the Spanish and Portuguese Jews have a translation in Spanish, which, as they generally understand, may be sufficient; but that not being the case in the British Dominions in America, has induced me to attempt a translation, not without hope that it may tend to the improvement of many of my brethren in their devotion." Admittedly, then, Pinto designed his work for American use; at all events, the objection of the Mahamad must have been to the language used by Pinto. We know how resolutely Bevis Marks clung to Spanish, and how reluctantly it abandoned some of the quaint uses made of it in announcements and otherwise.

" Some crudities there are in this translation, but few mistakes, and the style has a genuine devotional ring," says Mr. Singer. Pinto could not easily go wrong, seeing that he made use of Haham Nieto's " elegant Spanish translation." Dr. Gaster remarks that Pinto's rendering " rests entirely," as the author declares, on Nieto's. Pinto's exact words are: " In justice to the Learned and Reverend H. H. R. Ishac Nieto, I must acknowledge the very great advantage I derived " from Nieto's work. Mr. G. A. Kohut shares Mr. Singer's high opinion of Pinto's style. " The translation," he asserts, " seems to be totally free from foreign expressions, and is characterized throughout by a dignity and simplicity of diction which is on the whole admirable." With this favorable judgment all readers of Pinto will unhesitatingly concur. A remarkable feature which Pinto shares with Nieto is this: the translation appears without the Hebrew text. Commenting on the absence of Hebrew, Mr. Singer observes: " This fact would seem to show that there must have been an appreciable number of persons, who, for purposes of private worship at least, and perhaps also while in attendance at synagogue, depended upon English alone in their devotions." On the other hand, it is possible that, as Hebrew printing must have been costly in London and New York in the eighteenth century, the absence of the Hebrew may be merely due to the desire to avoid expenses. The translations may have been meant for use with copies of the Hebrew text printed in Amsterdam and elsewhere on the continent of Europe.

Pinto's book was small quarto in shape; it contained 191 pages. There are some peculiarities on the title-page, of which a facsimile may be seen in the *Jewish Encyclopedia,* vol. x, page 55: " Prayers for Shabbath, Rosh-Hashanah, and Kippur, or the Sabbath, the Beginning of the Year, and the Day of Atonements; with the *A*midah and Musaph of the Mo*a*dim, or solemn seasons. According to the Order of the Spanish and Portuguese Jews. Translated by Isaac Pinto. And for him printed by John Holt, in New York, A. M. 5526 "

(= 1766). It will be noted that Pinto indicates the *ayin* by the use of italics in the words *A*midah and Mo*a*dim. Also, though he employs the ordinary Sephardic term for the Day of Atonement (*Kippur* without the prefix of *Yom*), he does not translate the singular, but the plural, for he renders it the " Day of Atonements," which is not exactly a blunder (though the Hebrew *Kippurim* is, of course, really an abstract plural with a singular sense).

But who was Isaac Pinto? It is not at all clear. Some have hastily spoken of him as though he were identical with Joseph Jesurun Pinto, who was sent out by the London Sephardim to New York in 1758. The home authorities, at the request of the New York Congregation Shearith Israel, elected a Hazan, but the chosen candidate, " having since declined going for reasons unknown to us," writes the London Mahamad, through its treasurer, H. Men. da Costa, " we this day (June 7, 1758) proceeded to a second election, and our chois fell on Mr. Joseph Jesurun Pinto, who was examined by our direction and found very well versed in the reading of the Pentateuch and in the functions of a Hazan." This Hazan could do more: he was able, as Mr. Kohut shows, to write Hebrew, for in

October, 1760, he composed a prayer for recitation on the " General Thanksgiving for the Reducing of Canada to His Majesty's Dominions." The prayer was written in Hebrew, but printed in English, being translated by a " Friend of Truth." A note at the end of the booklet runs thus: " N. B. The foregoing prayer may be seen in Hebrew, at the Composer's Lodgings." Mr. Kohut adds: " Apparently original Hebrew scholarship was a curiosity in New York City in 1760."

A year before, Joseph Jesurun Pinto instituted the keeping of records as to those " entitled to Ashcaboth " (memorial prayers), and drew up a still used table of the times for beginning the Sabbath for the meridian of New York; he must have been a man of various gifts and activities.

What relation Isaac Pinto was to the Hazan we have no means of telling. Joseph's father was named Isaac, but this can scarcely have been our translator. An Isaac Pinto died in 1791, aged seventy; he may be (as Mr. Kohut suggests) the translator in question; in 1766 he would have been in his forty-fifth year. Steinschneider thought that he was identical with the author of a work against Voltaire (Amsterdam, 1762) and other treatises. " But," as Mr. Kohut argues, " this versatile author lived at Bordeaux, while our translator was in all probability a resident of New York." Mr. L. Hühner accepts this identification, and adds the possibility that this same Isaac Pinto was settled in Connecticut as early as 1748. More certain is it that Isaac Pinto is the same who appears in the earliest minute-book of the New York Congregation Shearith Israel as a contributing member and seat-holder (1740, 1747, and 1750).

Isaac Pinto was certainly living in New York in 1773. Ezra Stiles was president of Yale from 1778 till 1795, and in his diary he makes many references to Jews, as is well known from the publications of the American Jewish Historical Society. Under date June 14, 1773, Stiles has this entry: " In the forenoon I went to visit the Rabbi (Carigal)—discoursed on Ventriloquism and the Witch of Endor and the Reality of bringing up Samuel. He had not heard of Ventriloquism before and still doubted it. He showed me a Hebrew letter from Isaac Pinto to a Jew in New York, in which Mr. Pinto, who is now reading Aben Ezra, desires R. Carigal's thoughts upon some Arabic in Aben Ezra." Prof. Jastrow, from whose essay I cite the last sentence, adds: " As late as April 14, 1790, Stiles refers to a letter received from

Pinto, whom he speaks of as 'a learned Jew in
New York,' regarding a puzzling Hebrew inscription found by Stiles in Kent in the fall of 1789.
Unfortunately there is no other reference to this
supposed Hebrew inscription, on which Pinto was
unable to throw any light." Stiles does not seem
to have provided sufficient data. We would fain
know more of this Isaac Pinto. But the glimpses
we get of him are enough to satisfy us that he was
a man of uncommon personality.

MENDELSSOHN'S " JERUSALEM "

Of a hundred who discuss Moses Mendelssohn's conception of Judaism, perhaps barely five have read *Jerusalem,* the book in which that conception is most lucidly expressed. It is a common fate with certain literary masterpieces that they are read in their own day and talked about by posterity. The fame of Mendelssohn, moreover, underwent something like an eclipse during the last generation. To paraphrase what Antony said of Cæsar, but yesterday his word might have stood against the world; now, none so poor as to do him reverence.

The depreciation of Mendelssohn was due to two opposite reasons. For some time, though most Jews were unconscious of it, it was becoming obvious that there were two, and only two, thorough-going solutions of the Jewish problem for the modern age. The one may be termed religious liberalism, the other territorial nationalism. Now, Mendelssohn's views are in accord with neither of these tendencies. He was so far from being a territorialist—and I use that term in the widest sense— that he has been acclaimed and denounced as the father of assimilation. He was so remote from liberalism, that he has been acclaimed and de-

nounced as the founder of neo-orthodoxy. His
theory of life was that the emancipated Jew could
and must go on obeying under the new environment the *whole* of the olden Jewish law. This
is not possible! cry both the liberal and the
nationalist. Hence the liberal asserts one-half, the
nationalist the other half of the Mendelssohnian
theory. The liberal would modify the law, the
nationalist would change the environment. In
other words, instead of holding Mendelssohn in
low esteem, both sides ought to recognize that they
each derive half their inspiration from him.

And it is fortunate that Jews are, at this junc-
ture, coming to appreciate Mendelssohn all over
again. Our German brethren have just initiated
a capital series of little books which cost less than
a shilling each. The first of these " Monuments
of the Jewish Spirit " contains the *Jerusalem,* and
much else of Mendelssohn's work. Here one reads
again the words first penned by the Berlin Socrates
in 1783: Judaism knows nothing of a revealed
religion, Israel possessed a divine legislation.
" Thought is free," we can hear Mendelssohn
thundering—if so harsh a verb can be applied to
so gentle a spirit—" let no Government interfere
with men's mode of conceiving God and truth."

State and religion are separated as wide as the
poles. Israel has its own code, which in no way
conflicts with the State; still less does Israel seek
to impose that code on the State. Mendelssohn
did not believe that all men were destined to attain
to truth by the road of Judaism. " Judaism boasts
of no exclusive revelation of immutable truths in-
dispensable to salvation." Hence, too, " Judaism
has no articles of faith." It follows that not un-
belief was punished under the Jewish *régime,* but
contumacious disobedience. The Jew was never
commanded: believe this, disbelieve that; but do
this, and leave that undone. Judaism is the Jew's
way of attaining goodness, other people can attain
it in other ways. Not consonance but manifold-
ness is the design and end of Providence. " Religious union is not toleration, it is diametrically
opposed to it." Toleration consists rather in this:
" Reward and punish no doctrine; hold out no
allurement or bribe for the adoption of theological
opinions." How far in advance of his age Mendelssohn was! It took a full century after his
Jerusalem for England to abolish theological tests
at the universities, tests which indeed did " reward
and punish " doctrines. Mendelssohn goes on:
" Let everyone who does not disturb public happi-

ness, who is obedient to the civil government, who acts righteously towards his fellow-man, be allowed to speak as he thinks, to pray to God after his own fashion, or after the fashion of his fathers, and to seek eternal salvation where he thinks he may find it." No one, unless it be that earlier Jewish philosopher Spinoza, had ever put the case for toleration so cogently. Whether Mendelssohn's own principles are consistent with his further conclusion that once a Jew always a Jew, will ever be doubted. The Talmud (Sanhedrin 44a) had said: An Israelite, though he sin, remains an Israelite. Mendelssohn rather said: An Israelite has no right to sin. True, the world need not accept Judaism, but the Jew may never reject it. " I do not see," cries Mendelssohn, " how those who were born in the house of Jacob can, in any conscientious manner, disencumber themselves of the law. We are allowed to think about the law, to inquire into its spirit . . . . but all our fine reasoning cannot exonerate us from the strict obedience we owe to it." I am not now criticising Mendelssohn. I am trying to expound him. To live under the law of the State and at the same time to remain loyal to the law of Judaism is hard. But Mendelssohn went on: *Bear both burdens.* That assuredly is a counsel

181

which should be inscribed in golden letters over the portal of Judaism now, even though we may interpret the burdens differently in our different circumstances.

Mendelssohn's masterpiece includes much else. But what precedes ought to be enough to whet readers' appetites for the whole meal. On an occasion when I had a long talk with William James, I spoke to him of Mendelssohn, and he admitted that his own Pragmatic theories were paralleled by the *Jerusalem*. He promised to write on the subject, but death claimed him all too soon. Whether we agree with Mendelssohn or not, let us at least agree in appreciation of his genius. What he did, and what we do not do, is to face unflinchingly the discussion of fundamentals. Reading Mendelssohn is to breathe the fresh air. But there's the rub! *Read* Mendelssohn? How, if we know no German? It is deplorable that the *Jerusalem* is no longer accessible in English. I say no longer, because once it was accessible. And not once only, but twice.

In 1852, Isaac Leeser published an English version in Philadelphia. No wonder our American brothers still hold Leeser in such reverent esteem. He deserved well of the Jewry of his land. But

Leeser's was not the first English translation of
Jerusalem. In 1838, M. Samuels issued in two
volumes an English version in London; it was dedi-
cated to Isaac Lyon Goldsmid, and contained much
besides the *Jerusalem*. I know nothing of the
translator except one thing that he was not, and
another thing that he was. He was not a native
Englishman, and he was a good scholar. About a
dozen years earlier (1825) he had produced a
volume, entitled " Memoirs of Moses Mendel-
sohn " (what a pitfall that double *s* is to printers!
Throughout M. Samuels' earlier book an *s* is missing in the name; in the later publication it has been
recovered). Samuels asserts himself a " disciple
of the leading system of the work "; perhaps this
accounts for his enthusiasm, shown in his conscientious annotations, which are fragrant with genuine
Jewish thought. With very slight furbishing up,
Samuels' rendering could be re-printed to-day. One
of the most urgent needs of our age in English-
speaking lands is that Jews should once more become familiar with the thought of the eighteenth
century, and particularly of Mendelssohn. Like
many another of my generation, I was brought up
rather to decry him. I have learned better now,
and would fain urge others to a like reconsidera-
tion.

HERDER'S ANTHOLOGY

Johann Gottfried von Herder belonged to the school of Rousseau. The latter, from whom the French Revolution derived its philosophy, was enamored of the primitive and the ancient. Nature began far better than she became after man mishandled her. Herder (1744-1803) plays on the word "simplicity." He loved the Hebrew poetry because it was so spontaneous, so untainted by artificiality. Herder's work on the *Spirit of Hebrew Poetry* (1772-3) is fairly characterized by Graetz when he terms it epoch-making. Herder was among the first of the moderns to rouse interest in the Bible as literature. What his contemporary Lessing did in Germany for Shakespeare, Herder did for the Psalter.

Now Herder's treatment of ancient literature rendered a lasting service despite his fundamental misconception. What James Sully calls Herder's "excessive and sentimental interest in primitive human culture" prepared the way for the "genetic" theories of our time. He thoroughly realized the natural element in national poetry. He explained genius in terms of race. To him is due some part of the conception of a " Jewish culture," as formulated by present-day Zionists of Ahad ha-'Am's school. It is rather curious that while, on the one hand, Herder's theories helped national anti-Semitism, on the other hand, they gave suggestions to national Judaism. By laying undue stress on the natural, Herder exaggerated the national in the human spirit. In his early manhood Herder had thought of training as a physician. But he abandoned the idea because he could not endure the dissecting-room. When he came to discuss the world's genius he used the scalpel freely enough. His gorge rose against cutting up the body, but he felt no reluctance to dissect the spirit.

Earlier writers had overlooked the national element in the Bible. Herder saw in the Old Testament nothing but national songs. The thought often led him right. He strongly opposed, for instance, the mystic and allegorical interpretations of the Song of Songs. To him it was a love poem, the purest, most delicate love poem of antiquity (" den reinsten und zartesten Liebesdichtung des Altertums "). Hebrew literature was national, but it revealed its nationality under unique conditions, for it was marked by the "poetic consciousness of God." In all this Herder was magnificently right. But he could not leave well alone. In one of his latest essays he summed up the Hebrew poetry as distinguished indeed by religiosity, but also by simplicity ("kindliche Naivetät, Religiosität, Einfalt"). No term could be worse chosen. Hebrew poetry shows consummate art. If it conveys the sense of simplicity, it is because the poet's art so thoroughly conceals its workings. Herder made aesthetically the same mistake as Wellhausen perpetrated theologically. According to Wellhausen, the prophets of the eighth century before the Christian era suddenly appeared as an utterly new phenomenon on the Hebraic horizon, whereas, in truth, by the time we reach Amos we have got to a very advanced stage in the religious history of Israel. So, too, is it with the biblical poetry. It is, even in its earliest fragments, such as the Song of Deborah, a highly cultivated form. "Simplicity" is the last word to apply to it. It is powerful, it is sincere, but it is not naive. The Greek athlete who conquered at the Olympic games was robust, but he had gone through a long process of training. Vigor is not synonymous with artlessness. Trench wrote a charming book on the "use of

186

words." An equally entertaining book could be compiled on the " misuse of words." In such a book, a front place would be assignable to Herder's " simplicity."

What distinguished Hebrew poetry was not that element which it derived from the narrowing fetters of locality and epoch. Why is the Bible the most translatable book? Why has it been found the easiest of the great classics to re-express in the manifold tongues of man? Because it is so independent of the very qualities by which Herder sought to explain it! The poetry of Israel was " natural " and " national " in the sense that it corresponded to human nature, and was susceptible of interpretation in terms of every nationality. Over Herder's tomb was inscribed the legend " Licht, Liebe, Leben." Herder might have inscribed these or similar words over certain of the gems of Hebrew literature. " Light, love, life " are a truer characterization than " naiveness, religiosity, simplicity."

Graetz thought that, though Herder dreamed of the time when Jew and Gentile would understand and appreciate each other, he was ill-disposed to the Jews. He was, it is true, not one of those who fell under the spell of Moses Mendelssohn's per-

sonality. He was disinclined to subject himself to
the spell. When Mendelssohn sought Herder's
acquaintance, the latter received the proposal
coldly. This was not necessarily due to unkind-
ness. It seems to me that Herder, who much admired Lessing, was rather resentful of the close
intimacy between the hero and the author of
Nathan the Wise. Herder had no desire to form
one of a *ménage à trois.* As Graetz adds, Mendelssohn and Herder did come closely together
after Lessing's death. Herder, in one of his essays, dated 1781, the very year in which Lessing
passed away, pays Mendelssohn a pretty compliment, praising him as an exponent of Jewish ideals.

Herder's essay was prefixed to his " Anthology
from Eastern Poets " (*Blumenlese aus morgen-
ländische Dichtern*). Few of us remember that
the word *Anthology* corresponds exactly with
Blumenlese; it means a " collection of flowers."
(Compare Graetz's *Leket Shoshannim.*) Fore-
most among the floral graces of Herder's Oriental
garland are the famous selections made from
the Talmud and Midrash. Here, as elsewhere,
Herder was rather too inclined to treat the rabbinical legend and parable as " naive." He was,
moreover, a little patronizing to the Haggadists

when he declared that " people laughed at what they did not understand "—referring to the supposed grotesqueness of some of the rabbinic modes of expression. But he was happier when he described vandals like Eisenmenger as men who " rough-handled the butterfly, and who, mangling the beauteous creature between their coarse fingers, wondered that all they found on their hands was a particle of dust." No one has ever translated rabbinic parables so successfully as Herder. His very love for the unfamiliar stood him in good stead. He does not tell us whence he derived his knowledge of the originals. Probably it was in oral intercourse with Jews. Such a spelling of *Lilit* as *Lilis* looks as though he heard it pronounced by a German Jew.

Be that as it may, Herder enters into the spirit of the rabbinic apologues with rare understanding. He chose the subjects with judgment, and executed the renderings with felicity. There could have been nothing but love for Judaism in the man who thus selected and who thus translated. Graetz was unduly hard on him. It was quite possible for a man to be fond of Jews and yet not drawn to Mendelssohn. The last-named fascinated so many that he could afford to find one person antipathetic—if indeed he was so. Long before others took to a cult of the rabbinic wit and wisdom, long before Emanuel Deutsch startled the English world in October, 1867, by his question in the *Quarterly Review:* " What is the Talmud? ", Herder had introduced the German world to it, and had in part answered Deutsch's question by anticipation. From several points of view, therefore, Herder is of import for the Jewish student of nineteenth century history.

WALKER'S "THEODORE CYPHON"

Cumberland's play, *The Jew,* appeared in 1794, and two years later was published *Theodore Cyphon.* The author was George Walker, a bookseller of London and a prolific writer of novels. His works are a curious compound of wild melodramatic incident with comments, often shrewd enough, on social and political actualities.

Theodore Cyphon well represents Walker's method. The main plot is a tiresome story, told in retrospect, of Theodore's heroism and misfortunes in several walks of life, from the Minories to Arabia. He ends on the scaffold for an offence which was in truth his noblest act of chivalry. In between we have a quite able discussion on the cruelty of inflicting capital punishment in cases of mere robbery. The author concludes his Preface with the fear that readers may exclaim: " Well, it was very tragical; but I am glad the hero is settled at last." That, at least, is the sentiment of a modern reader.

This novel of Walker's, however, arrests attention by being set in a Jewish frame. The term frame is used advisedly, since the main narrative is independent of the setting.

The full title of the book is *Theodore Cyphon, or the Benevolent Jew.* There were two editions of it. The first came out in 1796, the second in 1823. Of the second edition the British Museum possesses a complete copy; of the first edition an imperfect example—consisting of the first of the three volumes—has recently been presented to the University Library, Cambridge. The " benevolent Jew " is one Shechem Bensadi, and he is drawn with more than sympathy. Shechem lends money at exorbitant rates to the improvident aristocracy, and devotes his gains to the relief of deserving unfortunates. Nay, his clients are not always deserving. When robbed, Shechem refuses to prosecute; he showers favors on those who treat him despitefully. His philanthropy is extended to Jew and Gentile alike. There is one remarkable scene in the fifth chapter, in which Shechem is shown in a large storehouse, surrounded by scores of poor Jews to whom he supplies goods, thus enabling them to earn a livelihood. In equally striking chapters Shechem plays the rôle of benefactor and friend to others than his own coreligionists.

The first edition of *Theodore Cyphon* was obviously suggested by Cumberland's success. Curiously enough, the sub-title, *The Benevolent Jew*, is used in the sheet concerning Cumberland's play printed in vol. vii of the *Transactions* of the Jewish Historical Society of England, p. 177. It is not improbable that the second edition of *Theodore Cyphon* was due to the popularity of Scott's *Ivanhoe*, which was published in December, 1819. There are not wanting some superficial parallels between Scott's masterpiece and Walker's earlier and more moderate production. Eve, Shechem's daughter, nurses Walker's hero, just as Isaac's daughter Rebecca nurses Scott's hero. The most interesting parallel—perhaps the only real one—is presented in two scenes, one in *Ivanhoe*, the other in *Theodore Cyphon*. The first is the occasion on which Rebecca sings her famous hymn. Scott describes his poem as a " translation " of a hymn with which the evening ritual of the Synagogue concluded. It is really an original composition inspired by various scriptural texts, and in its turn may have suggested some great lines in Kipling's *Recessional*. Is it possible that Scott's idea of Rebecca's hymn was suggested by Walker? For, in the second scene alluded to above, Eve, tco, is overheard singing a song to " music wild, yet so soft."

Walker gives us only the last stanza of Eve's song, which runs thus (p. 46 of vol. i of the 1796 edition) :

The wand'rers of Israel, through nations dispers'd,
　　Shall again dwell in safety, again rest in peace;
And the harp, that so plaintive our sorrows rehears'd,
　　Shall thrill with new pleasures, as pleasures increase;
The sweet, spicy shrubs, that wave over the hills,
　　Untouch'd by the simoom, eternally blow,
Frankincense and myrrh from their bosom distils,
　　And love shall attend on our path as we go.

Scott, of course, had other models beside Walker. Byron's *Hebrew Melodies* came out both with and without Nathan's musical accompaniment, in 1815, four years before *Ivanhoe* was written. It is curious, by the way, to note that Rudolf Eric Raspe, the original of the character whom Scott so mercilessly caricatures as Dousterswivel in his novel *The Antiquary,* was not only the author of *Baron Münchausen,* but was also the first translator into English of Lessing's *Nathan der Weise* (London, 1781). Scott does not seem to have been acquainted with Lessing's play, either in the original or in translation. Scott's indebtedness to Marlowe, on the other hand, has already been pointed out by the present writer.

194

Having drawn attention to the parallel between Walker and Scott, it will be useful to note an equally striking contrast. On pages 110-112 of *Theodore Cyphon* occurs the passage:

" His chief concern was for Eve, whom he saw, notwithstanding Theodore's supposed engagements, and the restrictions of religion, still encourage sentiments which sapped the foundation of her happiness, and which no expedient offered to remove, but by parting with its object, or suffering their marriage spite of religion and law.

" Though a Jew, skilled in the learning of the Talmud and Mosaic law, he was without those prejudices that attend on superstition. He saw clearly that, when those precepts were first instituted, they were designed as a prevention of communication between the Israelite and Heathen, lest by the influence and interchange of the softer sex, they might be led into the practice of idolatry. Yet now, taking up the argument in a religious way, the danger existed no longer; both Jew and Christian agreeing in the chief article of worship, though divided about what the understanding of neither can comprehend. In a civil light, man was created for the society of man. The distinction of kingdom and people were childish, and fit only to insult the understanding. But whilst he indulged himself in these speculations, he avoided hinting to Eve that there was a possibility she should ever become the wife of Theodore, that the unattainability of the object might blunt or destroy the ardour of hope: for however he might have wished for such a character (so far as observation could judge) as his son-in-law, under the present circumstances he could not have allowed it, had even the affections of Theodore been placed upon her, which he believed was far from the case, as the observation he had made when he entered his chamber abruptly, and the words, ' O Eliza,' which his daughter had heard, led him to conclude some prior engagement retained him."

The sequel shows that Theodore is already married to Eliza. With Walker's view, however, as to such a marriage, it is fruitful to compare the noble passage, on the same subject, with which Scott concludes the preface to the 1830 edition of *Ivanhoe:*

" The character of the fair Jewess found so much favour in the eyes of some fair readers, that the writer was censured, because, when arranging the fates of the characters of the drama, he had not assigned the hand of Wilfred to Rebecca, rather than to the less interesting Rowena. But, not to mention that the prejudices of the age rendered such an union almost impossible, the author may, in passing, observe that he thinks a character of a highly virtuous and lofty stamp is degraded rather than exalted by an attempt to reward virtue with temporal prosperity. Such is not the recompense which Providence has deemed worthy of suffering merit, and it is a dangerous and fatal doctrine to teach young persons, the most common readers of romance, that rectitude of conduct and of principle are either naturally allied with, or adequately rewarded by, the gratification of our passions, or attainment of our wishes. In a word, if a virtuous and self-denied character is dismissed with temporal wealth, greatness, rank, or the indulgence of such a rashly-formed or ill-assorted passion as that of Rebecca for Ivanhoe, the reader will be apt to say, Verily, virtue has had its reward. But a glance on the great picture of life will show, that the duties of self-denial, or the sacrifice of passion to principle, are seldom thus remunerated; and that the internal consciousness of their high-minded discharge of duty produces on their own reflections a more adequate recompense, in the form of that peace which the world cannot give or take away."

From the artistic point of view, Walker's novel has little merit. But it deserves to be better known from the historical point of view. It was another expression of the new attitude towards the Jew, which began to distinguish English letters in the latter part of the eighteenth century.

HORACE SMITH OF THE "REJECTED ADDRESSES"

Horace Smith and his brother James are famous as the joint authors of the most successful parody ever perpetrated. Drury Lane Theatre was re-opened on October 10, 1812, having been rebuilt after the fire which destroyed it some three years previously. The Committee advertised a competition for the best address to be spoken at the re-opening. It is easy to imagine what occurred. Masses of poems were sent in, and in despair all of them were rejected, and Byron was invited to write a prologue. It occurred to the Smiths to produce a series of parodies in the style of the poets of their day. They pretended that all, or most of them, had been candidates for the prize, and on the very day of the re-opening was published the volume of *Rejected Addresses,* which, conceived, executed, printed, and published within the space of six weeks, continues in the general judgment of critics the finest *jeu d'esprit* of its kind.

Interesting enough it would be to linger over the general aspects of this book. We must, nevertheless, resist the temptation to recall the marvellous imitations of that genial friend of ours, the author of *Ivanhoe*—or of that crabbed foe of Jewish emancipation, William Cobbett. Capital, too, is the skit on Thomas Moore. Eve and the apple come into that effusion as a matter of course. To Moore, Eve was as Charles' head to Mr. Dick. One could compile a fair-sized volume out of the Irish sentimentalist's allusions to the first pair in Paradise. Moore used the allusion seriously and humorously. In the *Lives of the Angels,* Adam is driven not from but into Paradise, for as Eve had to go, it would have been the reverse of bliss for him to be left behind in Eden. In another poem, Moore plays on the rabbinic suggestion that woman was made out of the man's tail, and so, comments the poet, man ever after has followed the original plan, and leaves his wife behind him whenever he can. Again and again, Moore in his poems claims close acquaintance with rabbinic lore, of which, in fact, he knew only a few scraps from second-hand sources.

So we might continue to glean thoughts from *Rejected Addresses*. It needs gleaning, because the direct references to contemporary Jews are very few. This negative point is not without interest. A dramatic squib nowadays would almost certainly have its hits against Jews. The Smiths only once refer to a Jew—the unfortunate Lyon Levi or Levy, who committed suicide by flinging himself over the London Monument. He was a merchant of Haydon Square, and the newspapers of January 19, 1810, record the event as having occurred on the previous day. It is not surprising that the incident should be fresh in men's minds when the Smiths wrote three years later. For after an interval of thirty-seven years, we again find an allusion to it in the *Ingoldsby Legends*. Levi was neither the first nor the last to precipitate himself from the summit of Wren's column; eventually the top was encaged, to bar others from a similar temptation.

It was remarked above that the *Rejected Addresses* were absolutely free from anti-Jewish gibes. Impossible would it have been for the Smiths to have acted otherwise. Horace, in particular, was an ardent admirer of Richard Cumberland, writer of *The Jew*, which at the end of the eighteenth century did so much to rehabilitate the Jews in English good-will. We can see Horace Smith's tendency, negatively, in one of his other poems. In the "Culprit and the Judge," he deals with a case of coin-clipping in medieval France.

As with all of Horace's verses, it is full of good points. The judge denounced as profanation the crime of filing the similitude of good King Pepin, and ordered the offender to be punished with decapitation. This is the clever reply of the culprit:

> " As to offending powers divine,"
> The culprit cried,—" be nothing said:
> Yours is a deeper guilt than mine.
> I took a portion from the head
> Of the King's image; you, oh fearful odds!
> Strike the whole head at once from God's!"

One wonders whether the author had ever heard of the closely parallel idea of the ancient Rabbi, who denounced the murderer as one who diminished the divine image in which man had been made. Observe, however, how Horace Smith refrains from making cheap capital out of the joke by describing the offender as a Jew. Smith knew the truth too well. He knew that, though some Jews were given to coin-clipping, there were many offenders who were not Jews. It is absolutely characteristic of Horace Smith that he should have refrained from libelling all Jews for the sins of some.

Horace Smith was, as already suggested, actuated in his philo-Semitism by knowledge. And this is the reason why, though his brother James wrote some of the best of the parodies in *Rejected Addresses,* this present article deals less with him than with Horace. For that the latter knew and understood Judaism can be demonstrated by the clearest evidence. In 1831 he published a prose volume, which ought to be better known to English Jews than it is. The title is " Festivals, Games, and Amusements, Ancient and Modern." The second chapter deals with the ancient Jews. It reveals an almost perfect insight into the Jewish conception of life. Only one or two passages require amendment to make it quite perfect. I need not expound, it will suffice to quote a single passage:

" It is worthy of remark that the government he (Moses) established, the only one claiming a divine author, was founded on the most democratical and even levelling principles. It was a theocratical commonwealth, having the Deity Himself for its King. Agriculture was the basis of the Mosaic polity; all the husbandmen were on a footing of perfect equality; riches conferred no permanent preeminence; there was neither peasantry nor nobility, unless the Levites may be considered a sort of priestly aristocracy, for they were entitled by their birth to certain privileges. But this is foreign to our purpose. The most distinguishing features of the government were the vigilant, the most anxious provisions made for the interests, enjoyments, and festivals of the nation; and that enlarged wisdom and profound knowledge of human nature, which led the inspired founder of the Hebrew commonwealth to exalt and sanctify the pleasures of the people by uniting them with religion, while he confirmed and endeared religion by combining it with all the popular gratifications."

When Sir Walter Scott saw the verses attributed to him in *Rejected Addresses*, he exclaimed: " I certainly must have written this myself, though I forget on what occasion." Some of us might say the same of certain of the phrases in the passage just quoted. The joyousness of Judaism has not been asserted with more sureness of touch by any Jewish writer than it was by Horace Smith. In another part of his book, he misconceived the attitude of the Pentateuch to the non-Jew, but otherwise he well understood Moses and the Law.

PART IV

Part IV

BYRON'S "HEBREW MELODIES"

No selection from Byron's poetry is complete unless it contain some of the "Hebrew Melodies." Matthew Arnold included five of the twenty-three pieces; Bulwer Lytton adopted them all. Swinburne, it is true, gave us a volume of selections without a Hebrew melody in it, but curiously enough he admits the verses beginning: "They say that Hope is happiness," which, it would seem, were intended for the melodies, though they do not appear among them. Nathan duly adds the lines to his collection, where they form the last item of the fourth and final "Number." The musician also includes "Francesca," and, on the other hand, omits the "Song of Saul before his Last Battle."

The "Melodies" first came out with settings by the Jewish musician, Isaac Nathan. The tunes, partly derived from the Synagogue, were not well chosen; hence, though the poems have survived, the settings are forgotten. In the same year (1815), John Murray also published the verses without the music. Before consenting to this step, Byron wrote to Nathan for permission to take it. He wished, he said, to oblige Mr. Murray, but " you know, Nathan, it is against all good fashion to give and take back. I therefore cannot grant what is not at my disposal." Nathan readily consented, and the volume of poems was issued with this Preface: " The subsequent poems were written at the request of the author's friend, the Hon. D. Kinnaird, for a selection of Hebrew melodies, and have been published with the music arranged by Mr. Braham and Mr. Nathan." In point of fact, Braham had nothing to do with the musical arrangement. Though his name is associated with Nathan's on the title page of the original edition, it is removed in the reprints.

It has been said above that the musical setting has not retained its hold on public taste. The Rev. Francis L. Cohen (in the *Jewish Encyclopedia,* vol. ix, p. 179) speaks of it as having " deservedly sunk into oblivion." I have recently had several of them played over to me, and my verdict is the same as Mr. Cohen's. In themselves the tunes are sometimes good enough, *Maoz Zur* appears among them. But the words and the airs rarely fit, and Nathan lost chances by ignoring the

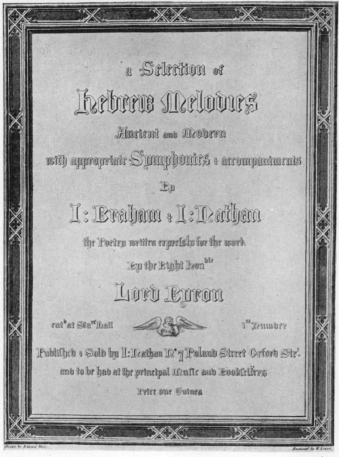

a Selection of

Hebrew Melodies

Ancient and Modern

with appropriate Symphonies & accompaniments

By

I: Braham & I: Nathan

the Poetry written expressly for the work

By the Right Honᵇˡᵉ

Lord Byron

entᵈ at Staʳˢ Hall   1ˢᵗ Number

Published & Sold by I: Nathan Nᵒ 7 Poland Street Oxford Strᵗ.

and to be had at the principal Music and Bookfellers

Price one Guinea

J Braham

TITLE-PAGE OF THE FIRST EDITION OF BYRON'S
"HEBREW MELODIES"

Sephardic music. Nathan's contemporaries had, however, a higher opinion of the work. Perhaps it was because the composer sang his songs so well; Braham does not seem to have included them in his repertoire. But Nathan's auditors were charmed by his renderings. Byron himself was most moved by " She Walks in Beauty "—to a modern ear Nathan's is a commonplace and inappropriate setting—and " he would not unfrequently join in its execution." The verses were really written for the tunes, and the poet often consulted the musician as to the style and metre of the stanzas. Nathan (in his *Fugitive Pieces,* 1829), records many conversations during the progress of the joint work. He tells us, for instance, how Byron refused to alter the end of " Jephtha's Daughter." As Nathan read the Scripture, and as many others also read it, Jephthah's daughter did *not* perish as a consequence of her father's vow; but Byron observed: " Do not seek to exhume the lady." On another occasion, Nathan was anxious to know what biblical passages were in the poet's mind when he wrote some of the verses, such as " O snatch'd away in beauty's bloom! " Byron vaguely answered: " Every mind must make its own reference." The local color of the poems, besides their substance, is in fact sometimes at fault. " Each flower the dews have *lightly* wet," is not a Palestinian touch; the dews there are remarkable for their heaviness.

At this point let us for a moment interrupt Nathan's reminiscences of Byron himself, and cite what he tells us of another famous poet's appreciation of the " Melodies." " When the Hebrew melodies were first published," says Nathan, " Sir Walter, then Mr. Scott, honoured me with a visit at my late residence in Poland Street. I sang several of the melodies to him—he repeated his visit, and requested that I would allow him to introduce his lady and his daughter. They came together, when I had the pleasure of singing to them ' Jephtha's Daughter,' and one or two more of the favourite airs: they entered into the spirit of the music with all the true taste and feeling so peculiar to the Scotch." Another admirer of Nathan's singing of the melodies was Lady Caroline Lamb, herself the author of what the conventions of the period would have termed " elegant verses." Once she wrote to Nathan: " I am, and have been, very ill; it would perhaps cure me if you could come and sing to me ' Oh Mariamne '—now will you? I entreat you, the moment you have this letter come and see me." The same lady translated for him a Hebrew elegy which he wrote on the death of his wife. Nathan must obviously have been an amiable companion and a charming renderer of his own music, or he would not have gained the applause of these distinguished judges.

As has been seen from the conversations recorded above, Byron and Nathan became very intimate in the course of their collaboration over the " Hebrew Melodies." It was this work that brought them together, though they were contemporaries at Cambridge about 1805, Byron being a student at Trinity College, and Nathan a pupil at Solomon Lyon's Jewish school in Cambridge town. But they naturally did not become acquainted then. Douglas Kinnaird (according to Mr. Prothero) introduced them to one another. Kinnaird was Byron's banker and Cambridge friend. This mention of Mr. Prothero reminds me that in his edition of Byron's Letters, he cites a note written by the poet to thank Nathan for a " seasonable bequest " of a parcel of *matsos*. Byron must have grown very attached to Nathan. An officious friend of the poet exhorted the musician to bring the melodies out in good style, so that his lordship's name " might not suffer from scantiness in their publication." Byron overheard the remark, and on the following evening said to Nathan: " Do not suffer that capricious fool to lead you into more expense than is absolutely necessary; bring out the book to your own taste. I have no ambition to gratify, beyond that of proving useful to you." The poet was, indeed, so indignant that he generously offered to share in the cost of production, an offer which Nathan as generously declined.

Readers of the " Hebrew Melodies " must have been struck by the appearance of *two* poems based on Psalm 137. Byron first wrote: " We sate down and wept by the waters," and later on another version beginning: " In the valley of waters we wept." Byron himself observed the duplication, and wished to suppress the former copy. It is well that he yielded to Nathan's importunities, for the first version is assuredly the finer. But the incident shows the close connection between the verses and the music. For Byron ended the discussion with these words: " I must confess I give a preference to my second version of this elegy; and since your music differs so widely from the former, I see no reason why it should not also make its public appearance."

Such being the close bond between poet and musician, it is all the more regrettable that the latter did not make a more competent use of his opportunity. A better fate befell the earlier collaboration which (in 1807) resulted in Thomas Moore's "Irish Melodies"—a title which suggested that given to Byron's series. Stevenson served Moore better than Nathan was able to serve Byron. Yet it seems a pity to leave things in this condition. Such poems as those already alluded to—and such others as "Saul," the "Vision of Belshazzar," and the "Destruction of Sennacherib"—all bear the clearest marks of their design; they were written to be sung, not merely to be read or recited. Jeffrey spoke of their sweetness; Lytton of their depth of feeling; Nathan himself realized that "Oh! weep for those" reaches the acme of emotional sympathy for persecuted Israel. Here, then, there is a chance for a modern Jewish musician. S. Mandelkern, in 1890, gave us a spirited translation of the verses into the Hebrew language. Let a better artist than Nathan now translate them musically into the Hebrew spirit.

COLERIDGE'S " TABLE TALK "

Coleridge was not master of his genius; his genius was master of him. In one place he speaks of the midrashic fancies about the state of our first parents as " Rabbinic dotages "; in another he laments, with Schelling, that these same rabbinic stories are neglected, and proceeds in his periodical, *The Friend,* to quote several with obvious approval. Again, he writes in one passage of the " proverbial misanthropy and bigotry " of Pharisaism; then, in another, he asserts, on the authority of Grotius, that the " Lord's Prayer " was a selection from the liturgy of the Synagogue.

The truth is that a large part of Coleridge's work is of the nature of table talk. His relative indeed published the poet's " Table Talk," but a good deal else in Coleridge belongs to the same category. His thoughts are, for the most part, *obiter dicta,* stray jottings, often stating profound truths, often expressing sheer nonsense. On the whole, he was not unkind to the Jews. He delivered many lectures on Shakespeare, but he never spoke on the *Merchant of Venice.* He alludes with contempt to the incident of the pound of flesh. Jacob, it is true, he regards as " a regular Jew " because of his trickiness; but he hastens to take the sting out of the remark by adding: " No man could be a bad man who loved as he loved Rachel."

Throughout we find, in Coleridge's remarks on the Jews and Judaism, the same mixture of conventional views and original judgments. He notes the theory that the Jews were destined to " remain a quiet light among the nations for the purpose of pointing out the doctrine of the unity of God," but spoils the compliment by the comment: " The religion of the Jew is, indeed, a light; but it is the light of the glow-worm, which gives no heat, and illumines nothing but itself." He can see in the Jew only love of money, yet he always found Jews " possessed of a strong national capacity for metaphysical discussions."

The last remark points to his personal familiarity with Jews. This was actually the case. " I have had," he says, " a good deal to do with Jews in the course of my life, although I never borrowed any money from them." He records several conversations with Jews, and does not hesitate to admit that he mostly got the worst of the argument. He argued with one Jew about conversion, and he cites the Jew's answer: " Let us convert Jews to Judaism first "—an epigram which has been a good deal repeated in other forms since 1830, when Coleridge first recorded it. On one occasion he accosted an " Old Clothes " man, and in a hectoring tone exclaimed: " Why can't you pronounce your trade cry clearly, why must you utter such a grunt? " The Jew answered: " Sir, I can say ' Old Clothes ' as well as you can, but if you had to say it ten times a minute, for an hour, you would say, ' Ogh clo' ' as I do now," and so he marched off. Coleridge confesses that he " felt floored." He was so much confounded by the justice of his retort, that, to cite his own words again: " I followed, and gave him a shilling, the only one I had."

Of one particular Jewish friend we know. Coleridge had a deep affection for Hyman Hurwitz, whom he terms " pious, learned, strong-minded, single-hearted." Afterwards Professor of Hebrew at University College, London, Hurwitz was, at the beginning of the nineteenth century, the head of the " Highgate Academy." He died in 1844, surviving Coleridge by ten years; the latter died at Highgate in 1834. Thus the poet and the Hebraist were neighbors as well as friends. Coleridge translated into poor English verse Hurwitz's feeble Hebrew elegy on the death of Princess Charlotte. He also contracted to prepare for the publisher, Murray, a volume of "Rabbinical Tales"; in this work Hurwitz was to collaborate with him. The fee was settled; it was to be two hundred guineas; but the arrangement came to nothing. Coleridge was rich in plans which he failed to accomplish. As an instance, let me cite what he says about an epic on the "Destruction of Jerusalem." "That," he declares, "is the only subject now remaining for an epic poem." Mark what follows: "I schemed it at twenty-five, but, alas! *venturum expectat*." Perhaps another remark of his explains why he never attempted the task. The subject of the destruction of Jerusalem, with great capabilities, has one great defect. "No genius or skill could possibly preserve the interest for the hero being merged in the interest for the event"—a profound sentiment.

Perhaps in no direction was Coleridge more in advance of his age than in his treatment of the ethics of the Pharisees. The Pharisees were, he contends truly, not a sect; they were, he puts it less aptly, the *Evangelicals* of their day. By that he means those who made religion the main concern of life; therein he is right, but the term is somewhat unhappily chosen. Yet not from one point of view. I have already cited Coleridge's opinion as to the Jewish sources of the "Lord's Prayer." He takes up a similar position with regard to the ethics of the Gospels in general. Here is a very remarkable concession: "The Being and Providence of the Living God, holy, gracious, merciful, the creator and preserver of all things, and a father of the righteous; the Moral Law in its utmost height, breadth, and purity; a state of retribution after death, the Resurrection of the Dead, and a Day of Judgment—all these were known and received by the Jewish people, as established articles of national faith, at or before the proclaiming of Christ by the Baptist." This is taken, not from the collection of "Table Talk" so named, but from the "Aids to Reflection" (Aphorism vii). Coleridge justifies his claim in behalf of the Jews by citing Leviticus 19. 2 and Micah 6. 8, finding the acme of morality in the command to be holy and in the prophet's answer to the question, "What doth the Lord require of thee?" Just so did Huxley choose Micah's saying: "To do justly, to love mercy, and walk humbly with thy God," as the last word of religion. To give the words of Huxley which cannot be repeated too often: "If any so-called religion takes away from this great saying of Micah, I think it wantonly mutilates, while if it adds thereto, I think it obscures, the perfect idea of religion." No two minds were more unlike than Huxley's and Coleridge's—the one the scientist, the other the metaphysician; the one the agnostic, the other the mystic. Yet they agreed in perceiving in the prophetic teaching a unique expression of basic moral truth.

BLANCO WHITE'S SONNET

Fear is natural by night. Man in the day-time is beset by foes; but while he can use his eyes, he has a sense of security. Something he can effect towards self-protection. But in the dark he feels helpless.

Hence it is natural that the Hebrew poets of the Midrash (on Psalm 92) have used as a theme Adam's first experience of the dark. There was no darkness on the first Friday after Creation. The primeval light, which illumined the world from end to end, was not quenched, though Adam had already sinned before night-fall of the day on which he was born. But the Sabbath came with the Friday's close, and the celestial rays shone on through the hours that should have been obscure. When, however, the Sabbath had passed, the heavenly light passed with it, and Adam, to his consternation, was unable to see. Would not the wily serpent choose this as a favorable moment for insidious onslaught? Then the light that failed in nature was kindled in man's intellect. Adam,

220

by the friction of two stones, cleverly made artificial light, and so could see again.

So runs one form of the Jewish legend. Another (I am summarizing both from Prof. Louis Ginzberg's *Legends of the Jews,* vol. i, pp. 86-89) expresses the thought differently. The primeval light does not figure in this version, but it is the normal sun that sinks before Adam's gaze on the Saturday night. Adam was filled with compunction. " Woe is me ! ", he exclaimed, " I have sinned, and because of me is the world darkened; because of me it will again return to a condition of chaos." So he passed the long vigil of the dark in tears, and Eve wept with him. But with the day he dried his eyes. For he saw the sun rise once more, and realized that the alternations of day and night were part of the divine order of nature.

In both these fancies Adam is much disturbed by his first experience of the dark, a guilty conscience made a coward of him. But not all Hebrew homilists rested in this attitude of fear. The author of the eighth Psalm is above all the poet of the night in its more uplifting aspects. He sees not the terror, but the illumination of the dark. The poet contemplates the heavens at night; he does not mention the sun, but " the moon and the stars " which God has ordained. " Unquestionably, the star-lit sky, especially in the transparent clearness of an Eastern atmosphere, is more suggestive of the vastness and variety and mystery of the universe." So writes Dr. Kirkpatrick on Psalm 8. 3, and he refers to an eloquent passage in Whewell's *Astronomy,* Book III, Chapter 3. Certainly those who have beheld the heavens on an Oriental night can conceive nothing more glorious than the spectacle, nor recall aught more wonderful than the Psalmist's description of it.

It was left to the theologian Blanco White to combine the two thoughts of fear and illumination, expressed in the Midrash quoted above and in Psalm 8, into an exquisite Sonnet. The author's name is queer enough. But though Joseph Blanco White (1775-1841) was born in Seville, he was an Irishman by descent. When the family settled in Spain, they translated the patronymic White into Blanco. On his coming to England, the theologian simply retained both forms of the name. As the writer in the *Dictionary of National Biography* recalls, Blanco White applied to himself the lines which occur in *Richard II,* Act i, scene 3. Nor-

folk, doomed to exile in a foreign land, thus
laments his fate:

> The language I have learn'd these forty years,
> My native English, now I must forgo;
> And now my tongue's use is to me no more
> Than an unstringèd viol or a harp.

Strange that this passage, of which only a small
part has been here quoted, has never been turned
into Hebrew, with a change in one single word of
the second line, by a Zionist. Yet more strange
that Blanco White, who thus deplored the fact that
his paternal English was not his native speech, has
given us one of the greatest poems in the English
language!

> Mysterious Night! when our first parent knew
>   Thee, from report divine, and heard thy name,
>   Did he not tremble for this lovely Frame,
> This glorious canopy of Light and Blue?
> Yet 'neath a curtain of translucent dew,
>   Bathed in the rays of the great setting Flame,
>   Hesperus with the Host of Heaven came,
> And lo! Creation widened in Man's view.
> Who could have thought such darkness lay concealed
>   Within thy beams, O sun! or who could find,
> Whilst fly, and leaf, and insect stood revealed,
>   That to such countless Orbs thou mad'st us blind?
> Why do we then shun Death with anxious strife?
> If Light can thus deceive, wherefore not Life?

It is indeed an exquisite thought. First we have Adam's fears as night falls. Then we have the reply, the antidote. The sun really conceals. Day shows us indeed insect and plant, but not the vast system of worlds which fill the heavens. It is night that brings to view the amazing extent of the stars, and unfolds the universe which the day had hidden. So death may reveal much that life conceals.

Coleridge pronounced this " the finest and most grandly conceived Sonnet in our language." The praise is not exaggerated. Yet it was written by one whose native tongue was Spanish, and who, though his career was extraordinary enough, never wrote another line in prose or verse that has lived. Single-speech Hamilton is joined in the realm of immortality by Single-Sonnet White. Written about a century ago, it lives and will go on living. As the writer from whom I drew the allusion to Shakespeare remarks: " Probably Blanco White will continue to be known by this Sonnet, when his other works, in spite of the real interest of his views, have been forgotten."

Great as the Sonnet is, it fails, however, to express the full significance of the eighth Psalm. The mazes and the wonders of the starry heaven above, unfolded as the sun sets by night, raise the question

" What is man? " that he should be of account when compared to these stupendous forces of nature. Yet, crowned with glory and honor, man is master of these forces. " The splendour of God set above the heavens is reflected in His image, man, whom He has crowned as His representative to rule over the earth " (Briggs). Contrasted though the glories be, the glory of man as creature is related to the glory of God as Creator.

DISRAELI'S "ALROY"

Benjamin Disraeli was one of the most truthful authors of the nineteenth century. To confuse his bombast with pose is to misunderstand him. When, therefore, he said of *Alroy* that it expressed his "ideal ambition," there is no reason to doubt his sincerity. Mr. Monypenny, whose judgment cannot be trusted in general, was right when he fully accepted Disraeli's statement on this point. Mr. Lucien Wolf had previously shown (in the splendid preface to his centenary edition of *Vivian Grey*) that "from start to finish, Lord Beaconsfield's novels are so many echoes and glimpses of the Greater Romance of his own life." Would that Mr. Wolf would give us an equally fine edition of *Alroy*.

For *Alroy* is a novel that deserves to live, and probably will live. From the first it has been better liked by the public than by the professional critics. Soon after the book first appeared in 1833, Disraeli wrote to his sister that he heard good reports as to the popularity of *Alroy*, and with characteristic "conceit," some may term it, though to

others it appears more like " insight," he added:
" I hear no complaints of its style, *except from the
critics.*" Mr. Monypenny has repeated the same
critical objections to the style. But such objections
have no real basis. *Alroy* often falls into rhythms
and even into rhymes. Why is this a defect in a
prose work? Dickens frequently followed the same
method, and in sundry impressive passages his sentences scan faultlessly. Are prose and verse so
absolutely divided from one another? If Molière's
bourgeois gentleman found that he had been speaking prose all his life without knowing it, so do we
sometimes speak verse without being conscious of
the fact. Do we not all " drop into poetry " on
occasion, in our ordinary speech in moments of
elevation? Moreover, the Oriental writers had
created a form in which prose and verse merge;
and Disraeli, treating an Eastern theme, might
easily have justified his choice of this very form,
beloved first of the medieval Arabs, and then
adopted by Hebrew contemporaries.

Then, as to the character of Alroy himself,
Disraeli's latest biographer says: " The real David
Alroy appears to have been little better than a
vulgar impostor, but Disraeli has idealised him
into a figure worthy to be compared with Judas

Maccabaeus." Mr. Monypenny borrowed this judgment (without acknowledgment) from the Rev. Michael Adler's able article in the *Jewish Encyclopedia*. I cannot myself assent to this verdict, though I appreciate the grounds on which it was reached. The whole thing turns on the application of the term " Pseudo-Messiah " to such characters. Why call them *false* ? There would be sufficient reason for applying the epithet if we had the clearest evidence that they were conscious rogues, exploiting their people's faith, and using their hope as a ladder towards personal ambition. We do not know enough of Alroy to assert this of him. Was Disraeli himself an impostor because he thought of himself as another redeemer of Israel? There is little doubt that Alroy is drawn from Disraeli himself, just as the Miriam of the story is modelled on the author's own sister. It is bad psychology to dub men of the Alroy type as impostors. Mr. Zangwill, in his *Dreamers of the Ghetto*—to my mind his most wonderful book— refuses to explain Sabbatai Zevi in this easy fashion. Graetz naturally so explained him, but it was precisely in such matters that Graetz was an unsafe guide. Are we to judge Messianic claims on the same principles as men judge political upheavals?

Treason never prospers, and for this reason:
That when it prospers no one calls it treason.

Is an enthusiastic believer in himself, as the instrument of a great emancipation, " pseudo " because he fails? Such explanations explain nothing.

Whatever be the truth as to the original Alroy—
and I repeat that the historical sources give us in-
adequate information as to his inner personality—
there is no room for doubting the character of
Disraeli's fictitious hero. Alroy is a thoroughly
sincere portraiture. Mr. Monypenny thought that
the story " never really grips us." It depends on
who the " us " are. A good many readers find
George Eliot's *Daniel Deronda* uninteresting. Yet
Daniel Deronda in Hebrew had a considerable success. Despite its queer mixture of ill-digested lore
and of genuine material derived from what Disraeli
termed the " erratic " Talmud, *Alroy* has a good
deal of Jewish spirit in it. In the many references
to the poetical elements of Jewish life, the sentiment rings true. This fact works backward.
Whence did the novelist derive this feeling for the
beautiful in Judaism except from his father?
Isaac Disraeli presents himself to us as a rather un-
sympathetic student of Judaism. In his books he

shows knowledge, but no feeling for the synagogue. It almost seems as though we do not see the real man in his books, and yet, after all, it may be doubted whether Benjamin inherited his Jewish idealism from his father. The latter did not at all approve of his son's Eastern journey. But Benjamin was consumed with the desire to visit Jerusalem, and he realized this passionate longing in 1830-1. In later life he said that he had begun *Alroy* before he left England. In the preface to *Alroy* he writes: " Being at Jerusalem in the year 1831, and visiting the traditionary tombs of the Kings of Israel, my thoughts recurred to a personage whose marvellous career had, even in boyhood, attracted my attention, as one fraught with the richest materials of poetic fiction. And I then commenced these pages that should commemorate the name of ' Alroy.' " I do not think that this statement contradicts his later assertion. When he says: " I *then* commenced," he may well be referring to his " boyhood."

Disraeli thoroughly enjoyed his stay in the Holy Land. He refused to admit that Athens was more impressive than Jerusalem. " I will not place this spectacle," he exclaims of the site of the ancient temple, " below the city of Minerva." Perhaps the most arresting detail in *Alroy* is the thirty-fifth note—the notes to the book, after the manner of Sir Walter Scott, are full of curious learning. He discusses the origin of coffee, the habits of the marten-cat, the art and furniture of the Orient, the sunset songs of Eastern maidens, the " Daughter of the Voice," the Persian hurling of the jerreeds (javelins) into the air, the practice of the basti- nado, the " golden wine " of Mount Lebanon, the alleged playing of chess before the date of the Trojan War, screens and fans made of the feath- ers of the roc, and the " tremulous aigrettes of brilliants " worn by persons of the highest rank. In all these directions Disraeli's learning and fancy run riot, and the result, sometimes as grotesque as a nightmare, is often successful in producing the required effect. But this thirty-fifth entry strikes a more personal note. Let us read it in his own words, remembering, however, that the Mosque of Omar was certainly in existence in Alroy's day: " The finest view of Jerusalem is from the Mount of Olives. It is little altered since the period when David Alroy is supposed to have gazed upon it; but it is enriched by the splendid Mosque of Omar, built by the Moslem conquerors on the supposed site of the Temple, and which, with its gardens, and arcades, and courts, and fountains, may fairly be described as the most imposing of Moslem fanes. *I endeavored to enter it at the hazard of my life.* I was detected and surrounded by a crowd of turbaned fanatics, and escaped with difficulty; but I saw enough to feel that minute inspection would not belie the general character I formed from it from the Mount of Olives. I caught a glorious glimpse of splendid courts, and light airy gates of Saracenic triumph, flights of noble steps, long arcades, and interior gardens, where silver fountains spouted their tall streams amid the taller cypresses."

Here we, too, have a " glorious glimpse " into one-half of the real Disraeli—here and in *Tancred;* for the other half we must study his political novels. *Vivian Grey,* so Disraeli himself said, expressed his " practical," as *Alroy* expressed his " ideal," ambition. And one final word. I have said nothing of the plot of *Alroy.* I assume it to be familiar to my readers. If it be not, they can easily make good the omission. I have no fear that this story of a twelfth century—shall I call him " hero " or " impostor "?—will fail to grip. For it is more than a story, it is—to use that over-worked phrase— also a " human document."

ROBERT GRANT'S " SACRED POEMS "

When Gibbon wrote the famous fiftieth chapter of the *Decline and Fall,* he was suspected of being a Mohammedan, because he dealt leniently with the Arab religion. Edwin Arnold was half believed to be a Buddhist, because his *Light of Asia* idealized the saint of India. But Robert Grant was never called a Jew, despite the fact that he was the champion of Jewish rights in Parliament. Grant was too genuine a Christian for anyone to doubt his orthodoxy. The same man who brought in the 1830 Bill to remove Jewish political disabilities was the author of some of the most popular hymns of the Church.

Yet, as though to show the Hebrew spirit of this non-Hebraic friend of the Hebrews, the best of his poems were written on Hebrew themes. Sir Robert Grant died in India in 1838; he had gone out as governor of Bombay. In the following year, his brother, Lord Glenelg, published Grant's *Sacred Poems.* It was a small book, containing in all only a dozen items. But it had a great vogue, and

233

some of the poems found a place " in almost every collection of devotional verse," as the children of the author proudly claim in the preface to the 1868 edition. Grant would have been especially gratified, one may feel certain, had he been able to anticipate that his translation of parts of Psalm 104 would be adopted in such Jewish compilations as the Services for Children drawn up for use in the New West End Synagogue, London.

A charming poem did Grant write on the text: " Whom have I in heaven but Thee? And there is none upon earth that I desire in comparison of Thee " (Psalm 73. 25). Earth is beautiful with its " woods that wave," its " hills that tower," and " Ocean rolling in his power "; human friendship is a " gem transcending price," while love is a " flower from Paradise,"

> Yet, amidst this scene so fair,
> Should I cease Thy smile to share,
> What were all its joys to me?
> Whom have I on earth but Thee?

And so with heaven, where " beyond our sight," there " rolls a world of purer light," with its unclouded bliss, its union of severed hearts, where " immortal music rings " from " unnumbered seraph strings."

O! that world is passing fair;
Yet if Thou wert absent there,
What were all its joys to me?
Whom have I in heaven but Thee?

The poem might have closed there, perhaps a stronger writer would have suppressed the thin stanza. But while it detracts from the virility of the verses, it adds measurably to their tenderness.

Lord of earth and heaven! my breast
Seeks in Thee its only rest;
I was lost, Thy accents mild
Homeward lur'd Thy wandering child;
I was blind; Thy healing ray
Charm'd the long eclipse away;
Source of every joy I know,
Solace of my every woe,
O if once Thy smile divine
Ceas'd upon my soul to shine,
What were earth or heaven to me?
What have I in each but Thee?

Almost as good in idea, though not so perfect in form, is Grant's set of verses on Psalm 94. 12: "Blessed is the man whom thou chastenest."

Enchanted with all that was dazzling and fair,
I followed the rainbow—I caught at the toy;
And still in displeasure Thy goodness was there,
Disappointing the hope, and defeating the joy.

The divine goodness is seen in man's disappointments, when the fulfilment of hope would have been loss, not gain.

On the whole, however, Grant is less successful when writing to a text than when paraphrasing a context. His renderings of certain Psalms are among the best attempts of the kind. This praise applies to his version of Psalm 49; less unreservedly to his adaptation of Psalm 2. In rendering Psalm 71, Grant gave sentiment too loose a rein. Addison had translated the opening verses of Psalm 19, beginning " The spacious firmament on high." Grant composed what he called " a sequel or counterpart " to Addison's hymn, corresponding to the latter portion of Psalm 19 as Addison's fragment corresponds to the earlier portion. Grant's supplement ends thus:

> Almighty Lord! the sun shall fail,
> The moon forget her nightly tale,
> And deepest silence hush on high
> The radiant chorus of the sky;
> But, fixed for everlasting years,
> Unmoved amid the wreck of spheres,
> Thy word shall shine in cloudless day,
> When heaven and earth have passed away.

This is fine, but Grant here hardly bears comparison with Addison: it is the fate of sequels to prove inferior to their forerunners. There is noth-

ing in Grant's version to equal Addison's close,
where the sun, moon, and stars are

> Forever singing as they shine,
> "The hand that made us is divine."

On the other hand, Grant falls very little below
Milton in his imitation of part of Psalm 84. I
must find room to quote it in full.

> How deep the joy, Almighty Lord,
> Thy altars to the heart afford!
>   With envying eyes I see
> The swallow fly to nestle there,
> And find within the house of prayer
>   A bliss denied to me!
>
> Compelled by day to roam for food
> Where scorching suns or tempests rude
>   Their angry influence fling,
> O, gladly in that sheltered nest
> She smooths, at eve, her ruffled breast,
>   And folds her weary wing.
>
> Thrice happy wand'rer! fain would I,
> Like thee, from ruder climates fly,
>   That seat of rest to share;
> Opprest with tumult, sick with wrongs,
> How oft my fainting spirit longs
>   To lay its sorrows there!
>
> Oh! ever on that holy ground
> The cov'ring cherub Peace is found,
>   With brooding wings serene;

And Charity's seraphic glow,
And gleams of glory that foreshow
  A higher, brighter scene.

For even that refuge but bestows
A transient tho' a sweet repose,
  For one short hour allowed;—
Then upwards we shall take our flight
To hail a spring without a blight,
  A heaven without a cloud!

Had Grant ever studied rabbinic commentaries? For this is the very use made of the eighty-fourth Psalm in the Midrash. The earthly pilgrimage leads to the heavenly Zion.

I have used for this poem space which some readers may have expected me to reserve for the best of all of Grant's renderings, that of portions of Psalm 104. In this Grant not only does not fall below the greatest of his predecessors—Henry Vaughan—but he transcends even that master's work. It is true that Vaughan renders the whole of this long Psalm literally, whereas Grant merely paraphrases a few verses. But none the less, Grant's " O Worship the King " is a superb reproduction of the Psalmist's spirit. As not uncommonly happens with Grant, he falls off towards the end, and his sixth verse is nowadays justly deleted when the rendering is used liturgically. Nothing, however, could be more exquisite than these stanzas:

> The earth with its store
>   Of wonders untold,
> Almighty! Thy power
>   Hath founded of old:
> Hath 'stablished it fast
>   By a changeless decree,
> And round it hath cast,
>   Like a mantle, the sea.
>
> Thy bountiful care
>   What tongue can recite?
> It breathes in the air,
>   It shines in the light;
> It streams from the hills,
>   It descends to the plains,
> And sweetly distils
>   In the dew and the rain.

One wonders at his versatility. He could draft a bill for parliament deftly, and then indite such verses as those quoted. There is, indeed, something akin to the Hebrew genius in the English. For David, too, could govern, and in the intervals of ruling meditate the Psalms which make so eternal an appeal. On Robert Grant, the advocate of Jewish rights, there had, indeed, fallen a portion of the Davidic spirit.

GUTZKOW'S " URIEL ACOSTA "

Twice within my recollection there were hopes of the production of *Uriel Acosta* on the English stage. Soon after Sir Hall Caine published the *Scapegoat*—that noblest of recent tales with a " Jewish " plot—Sir Herbert Tree was present with the novelist at a Maccabean banquet. On that occasion Sir Herbert, adopting a suggestion of my own, announced that he had proposed to Mr. Zangwill the office of preparing *Uriel Acosta* for His Majesty's Theatre. Nothing has come of it. Some years before, that competent actor, Mr. A. Bandmann, was lessee of the Lyceum for a time. He had often played the part of Uriel in Germany with success, and he had an English version made. It was not performed, but the plan was so far fruitful that Mr. H. Spicer's adaptation was published.

It is a workmanlike but undistinguished rendering. It introduces mistakes for which Gutzkow is guiltless (such as the barbarism *Sanhedrim*), and it omits points which make up Gutzkow's merit. Curious, for instance, is it that the English version should obscure the line which so lingers in the mind of the reader of the original, the line in fact most often quoted of everything that Gutzkow wrote. I refer, of course, to the old Rabbi's constant comment on Uriel's heresies. These, urged the Rabbi, are as old as old; it has all happened before (" Alles ist schon einmal dagewesen "). It is a striking variant on Solomon's epigram, " there is nothing new under the sun " (Ecclesiastes 1. 9), and it drones through the recantation scene with fine dramatic effect. Far superior to this English version is the Hebrew rendering published by Salomo Rubin in 1856.

The actual facts about Uriel Acosta are soon told. His was an arresting personality, but his importance has been much overrated. Acosta would have been deservedly forgotten but for the similarity between his career and that of another Amsterdam Jew of the same period—Baruch Spinoza. Both came into conflict with the synagogue, both were excommunicated. But there the resemblance ends. In Gutzkow's play, Uriel proclaims himself sufficient unto himself (" Mir selber bin ich eine ganze Welt "). This is just what Spinoza was, just what Uriel was not. Gutzkow represents Uriel as a youth at the time of his suicide. But he was certainly over fifty, and more probably was nearer sixty. He shot himself in 1647; and as it appears that he was born in Oporto in 1590, he must have been fifty-seven at the moment of his tragic end. Uriel (or Gabriel as he was then named) was the scion of a Marano family, and in 1617 contrived to escape to Holland, where he resumed Judaism. But he was no more contented with his ancestral religion than he had beeen with the creed to which he had compulsorily conformed. He advocated a purely deistic philosophy, was excommunicated by the synagogue, recanted, again defied the authorities, was again excommunicated, and finally underwent the degradation of a public penance, after which he put an end to his troubled life. Uriel's misfortune was that, though, like Spinoza, he was unable to go with the mass in its beliefs, yet unlike Spinoza, he was unable to stand alone.

Gutzkow was attracted to the subject by his own devotion to freedom. In the stormy movements which culminated in the outbreaks of 1848, Gutzkow was directly implicated. He was born in 1811, and, when barely twenty, suffered imprisonment as a leader of the " Young Germany " party. Besides, Gutzkow had many close Jewish friends, among them Berthold Auerbach, who, perhaps, introduced Uriel Acosta to his notice. When Gutzkow wrote his play on the subject, Europe was on the eve of revolution. It is significant, in face of the anti-Semitism which really originated on the failure of the Liberals, that Gutzkow selected, in 1847, a Jewish *mis-en-scène,* in order to depict the struggle between the old order and the new. And it is impossible to refuse admiration to the insight and skill which enable the author, while obviously sympathizing with the new, to treat the old with justice and even with tenderness. The characters are all types. Menasseh, father of Judith, is the fair-dealing merchant, accepting the current religion of his people without enthusiasm for or against its demands. Judith, the heroine, more or less betrothed to Jochai, the villain of the piece, is vaguely susceptible to the newer ideas of her tutor and lover Uriel. Jochai is a rather conventionally drawn rascal. But the strength of the play is the contrast, on the one hand, between Uriel and the Rabbis, and, on the other, between the various schools of Rabbis among themselves. Da Silva has the tolerance of uncertainty as to his own position, Akiba has the broad generosity which comes from confidence in his old-world loyalty.

The scenes between Uriel and Silva, and between the former and Akiba would make a success on any stage. " May you never repent of this repentance," cries Da Silva to Akiba when there is talk of Uriel's recantation. There is strong emotional interest in this recantation. Shall Uriel recant for Judith's sake? Hardly. But he cannot resist the appeal of his blind mother. " I tremble before thy sightless eyes; shut thine eyes, mother! Yea, I will do it."

The close is tragic. Both Judith and Uriel perish at their own hands. But the tragedy did not end there. Mention has been made of Da Silva. If Uriel is the counterpart of the talmudic arch-heretic, Elisha ben Abuyah, then is Da Silva the reincarnation of Elisha's contemporary Meir. Who has not wept over the heart friendship but mind estrangement of these two men? Da Silva stands in the same relation to Uriel. He hates the heresy, but loves the heretic. Uriel himself uses words which sum up the situation. " Love or Truth? What if the heart be wiser than the mind?" Spinoza (who was really fifteen years of age when Uriel died) flits across the scene as a little boy, strewing flowers and wondering why people wonder at his childish thoughts. Uriel bids him " Keep thy soul's secret and so find peace." This is perhaps the most tragic incident in the play, though the dramatist contrives to relieve the tension by the simple beauty of the Spinoza interlude.

Still, however, the whole of the tragedy has not yet been told. For Hermann Jellinek has not yet been named. Indeed, *three* remarkable Jellinek brothers now come on the scene. In 1847 two little works appeared on Gutzkow's *Uriel.* The one (*Elischa ben Abuya*) was written by Adolf Jellinek, then the youthful preacher of Leipzig, afterwards the famous pulpit orator of Vienna. The other was *Uriel Acosta's Leben und Lehre,* and its author was Hermann Jellinek (younger than Adolf by a couple of years). The booklet was inscribed to a third brother, Moritz. Now Hermann Jellinek was roused to a heated indignation by Gutzkow's " fictions " about Uriel. Uriel was no lovelorn boy, but a middle-aged philosopher; he died not for loss of Judith, but as a martyr to truth. Hermann Jellinek in so many words sees his own prototype in Acosta; less than a year later he at all events shared his hero's tragic end; but under more dignified circumstances. What the historical Uriel Acosta lacked, Hermann Jellinek possessed in over measure—the quality of determination. Hermann was a revolutionary, and took part in the Viennese rising of 1848, being twenty-six at the time. He does not seem to have actually resisted the troops, but he was court-martialled, and sentenced to death. His friends made every effort to save him, but he was relentless. Nothing could move him to present a conciliatory front to the authorities. In this at least he could be no Uriel! Recant? No! "Shoot me," he cried, "but ideas cannot be shot." They shot him, and his ideas may be found in two or three volumes, of which dusty copies occur in a few libraries. I have some of them on my table as I write. It is not easy to say which is the greater tragedy, Acosta's or Jellinek's; but for the moment at least let Jellinek have his way. For an hour we have resurrected, if not his ideas, at all events his name.

GRACE AGUILAR'S " SPIRIT OF JUDAISM "

Known to the many for her novels, Grace Aguilar is known to the few for her *Spirit of Judaism*. The book passed through a real adventure, quite as exciting as the fictional fortunes of any of her romantic heroes. Somewhat before 1840, Miss Aguilar wrote to Isaac Leeser, of Philadelphia. She had, in 1839, read the Rabbi's first published sermons—his Bible was yet to come. She asked him " to undertake the editorial supervision of her manuscript work on the *Spirit* of our religion." Leeser courteously responded to the request. " I shall readily be believed," he wrote in 1842, " that I felt truly happy that such a demand had been made upon me; and I accordingly offered my services to do as I was desired." Miss Aguilar completed the book, but chance decreed that it was not to reach its goal. She sent it out to America " through a private channel," and it never came to Leeser's hands. Such a mishap did not thwart so ardent and industrious a girl—she was not much over twenty at the time. She accordingly proceeded to re-write it "from her original sketches," made in 1837. On the second occasion fortune was more kind, though the book encountered some further delays before it appeared, in 1842, in America.

A second edition—much inferior from the point of view of " get-up "—was published in 1849, again in Philadelphia. The second issue was No. xiii of the *Jewish Miscellany* of the original Jewish Publication Society. The book was never printed in England. My own introduction to it was curiously made. Being deeply interested in the new plans for teaching Hebrew, I wrote (in 1903), a preface to a book on the Yellin method. I showed the proof of my essay to the late Rev. S. Singer, whereupon he remarked: " Grace Aguilar said much the same thing more than half a century ago." And so, indeed, she did. She saw that Hebrew must be taught naturally, that the language must be made to " engage a child's fancy," by first of all introducing to it familiar Hebrew words from the child's every-day life. Glad was I to find this anticipation of modern opinion, and I cited it fully.

From that time I have, for other reasons, grown very fond of the book—of which I possess the 1849

GRACE AGUILAR

reprint. It is so delightfully fresh and young, so confident and enthusiastic. Moreover, there is something entertaining in Leeser's conception of his editorial function. Not that he could well help himself. He was almost compelled to apply a wet blanket to her fire. She had expressly invited him to confine himself to removing obscurities and appending the necessary notes. " The chief point of difference between Miss Aguilar and myself," says Leeser, " are her seeming aversion to the *tradition*, and her idea that the mere teaching of formal religion opens the door to the admission of Christianity." On the second point, Leeser's answer is effective. If, through unintelligent teaching, ceremonial religion degenerates into a burden, then the outcome is more likely to be disregard for the old than regard for a new faith. " Indifference is a far greater enemy to us than conversion," said Leeser in 1842, and assuredly we can use identical words now. It is not so clear, however, that Leeser was equally successful in meeting Miss Aguilar on the problem of tradition. She was very emphatic in her desire to base Judaism on the Bible, but she was only verbally, not spiritually, a Karaite. She often uses the very language of tradition, and in one place says: " The religion of no Hebrew is perfect, unless the form be hallowed by the spirit, the spirit quickened by the form. The heart must be wholly given to the Lord, yet still the instituted form must be obeyed." Miss Aguilar probably objected to the minutiae of pietism—in the ritual sense—when she spoke of tradition; she had no philosophical conception of it. Leeser could hardly be expected to set her right; he was as little of a mystic as she was.

No doubt, however, she was to this extent an anti-traditionalist that she thought the Bible in itself an all-sufficient basis for Judaism. Her book is cast in the form of a commentary on the Shema'— in fact, it is called " Shema Israel, the Spirit of Judaism." She begins by expounding the unity of God; she shows that it is the real difference between Synagogue and Church; and then ends her chapter with a passionate plea for friendly intercourse between Jew and Christian on the basis of frank and unashamed profession of Judaism by the former. She was absolutely right. It is not merely the only honest, it is also the only stable basis for such intercourse.

To Grace Aguilar, Moses was " the mouth of God " (that is her own phrase). There is nothing between a theory of verbal inspiration and the belief that Moses "invented" and " presumed on the ignorance and superstition of the rescued nation." With a feminine love of italics she contends that " we *must* believe God framed *every law* mentioned in the Mosaic books or *none*." How crude this sounds! On the one hand, it cuts off all thought of inspiration before Moses, on the other, all thought of it after the close of the scriptural canon. It would have seemed to her almost blasphemous to regard Hillel as animated with the same spirit of God that moved Haggai. She dismisses the " Oral Law " in an aside. " The Bible is the foundation of religion." Miss Aguilar goes on to complain that English Bibles were not found in Jewish homes. But the explanation is easy. In those days it was impossible to find an acceptable English Bible for Jewish use. The Authorized Version was marred not only by Christological renderings, but also by the Christological insertions of the headings to the chapters. Before the publication of the Revised Version it had become possible to obtain an Anglican edition without the headings. But I doubt whether that was the case so early as 1842. Moreover, Jews have always been slow to acknowledge that the *Hebrew* Bible was insufficient. There was much that is creditable in this reluctance to face facts; though there was also much that was dangerous.

It is impossible to do justice in a brief article to the intense love of Judaism shown in Miss Aguilar's book. She pleads for the religion with persuasive eloquence; it must appeal to the heart and the reason; it must permeate the home; it must regulate life. She would have family prayers daily. To this topic she returns over and over again. " The youthful members of a little domestic congregation would look back with warm emotion, in after years, to that period when, with their brothers and sisters, they thronged around their parents to listen to the word of God, and made known their common wants together." But the thought that dominates her whole book is the perfect truth and sufficiency of Judaism. It only needs to be known to be preferred to every possible alternative. No Jew can ever become lukewarm if he understands his religion. But he must understand its spirit. " We know that they who depart from the faith of their fathers are ever those reared in the severest obedience to mere forms." Whereupon Leeser in his note comments: " This is certainly a sweeping clause though there is a great deal of truth in it." He adds that the fault " does not lie in the *forms*, but in the absence of *spiritual* education." That is clearly the reason why Miss Aguilar called her book " The Spirit of Judaism." She was no foe to forms as such. She strongly defends the dietary laws, in the very chapter whence the last quotation was taken. *Obedience* is the term writ large on every page; but so is *belief*. When Judaism is believed in and obeyed, then will redemption be nigh, release from captivity at hand, and the advent of the Messiah approaching. But how movingly she says it in her own fiery words!

ISAAC LEESER'S BIBLE

The twenty years around the middle of the nine-teenth century witnessed the preparation of several Jewish translations of the Bible. Moses Mendels-sohn had shown the way in the previous century; he did not, however, produce a *complete* German Bible. This was done with success by a body of scholars led by Zunz (Berlin, 1838). Ludwig Philippson, in the very next year, began an enter-prise the accomplishment of which occupied him till 1856. His edition was not only annotated; it was also adorned with illustrations. In 1875 the Philippson Bible came out anew with the Doré pictures.

As for English versions by Jews, David Levi edited the Pentateuch in 1787. But, to pass over certain publications of separate books, no complete Bible appeared in England from a Jewish hand un-til the issue of Benisch's version (1851-56). This was a melancholy affair. Real and original scholar-ship is shown in every page. He claimed for his rendering " fidelity, uniformity and independence." But he had no sense for English style. He un-

ISAAC LEESER

(From a Painting by Solomon Nunez de Carvalho)

necessarily and grotesquely altered the familiar words of the Authorized Version. Hence, one is bound to speak of this monument of learning and earnestness as " melancholy "; it might so easily have been acceptable. His corrections of the Authorized were often necessary. Thus, in the Ten Commandments he rightly put " Thou shalt not murder " for the current " Thou shalt not kill." The Revised Version made the same correction. So, too, he was right when, for historical reasons, he made a change in Leviticus 23. 15. In the Authorized Version this runs: " And ye shall count unto you from the morrow after the Sabbath." But by the Jewish tradition the Feast of Weeks is not counted from a Saturday but from the first day of Passover—on whatever day that happens to fall. Hence Benisch substituted: " And ye shall count unto you from the morrow after *the day of rest*." Naturally, too, he corrected certain dogmatic prejudices of the Anglican Version.

Curiously enough, Isaac Leeser leaves " Thou shalt not kill " uncorrected. But he was vigilant with " the morrow after the Sabbath," for which he substitutes " the morrow after the holy day." On the other hand, he retained the word " Sabbath " (where the Hebrew has *Shabbaton*) applied to the first and eighth days of Tabernacle, *e. g.*, Leviticus 23. 39. This, however, he altered in his later editions to *a rest;* Benisch has *strict rest.* The Revised Version has a similar correction: *solemn rest.*

It is not my purpose to compare Leeser's Version with others. From the hour when his " Law of God " appeared in Philadelphia, in 1845, Leeser's Pentateuch won the affectionate regard of American Jews. The Pentateuch was issued in octavo, in Hebrew and English; the whole of the Bible came out in quarto, in English alone, towards the end of 1853. From that time it has been often reprinted in varying forms, simply and in editions *de luxe.* But it is not the printers who made the book popular, though I must remark that, despite the small public support the enterprise secured, the 1845 Leeser Pentateuch is a beautiful specimen of the printer's art. What made the book was the people's growing love for Leeser. Can higher praise be given, can a finer fate be wished, than that a man's book shall live in his brethren's hearts because of him?

This is not the time to criticise Leeser's work. Like Benisch, he had no feeling for English style. He could, in the twenty-third Psalm, alter the won-

derful melody of " He maketh me to lie down in
green pastures," into " In pastures of tender grass
he causeth me to lie down." He could take the
haunting rhythm of Job's " There the wicked cease
from troubling, there the weary are at rest," and
give us " and where the exhausted weary are at
rest," which is no nearer the literal Hebrew (" the
wearied in strength "), and is incomparably farther
from its beauty. Or again, the felicitous opening
lines of the nineteenth Psalm, " The heavens de-
clare the glory of God; and the firmament sheweth
his handiwork," become in Leeser " The heavens
relate the glory of God; and the expanse telleth of
the works of his hands." It is this more than anything else that made it impossible for English Jews
to use Leeser's Bible. Revision of Leeser on
scholarly grounds was also necessary, no doubt.
Thus, in his rendering of Esther 6. 8, where
Haman suggests the details of the pageant in behalf of the man whom the king delighteth (why
did Leeser substitute *desireth ?*) to honor, Leeser
has: " Let them bring a royal apparel which the
king hath worn, and a horse on which the king
hath ridden, and let there be placed a royal crown
on his head." But, as Ibn Ezra had in part already pointed out (as Leeser notes), and as we

know to be almost certainly the case, the crown was for the *horse's* head. In the Revised Version the passage runs: "Let royal apparel be brought which the king useth to wear, and the horse that the king rideth upon, and on the head of which a royal crown is set."

Naturally, in what precedes I have turned to familiar passages. My comments only touch the fringe of the problem of Bible revision. In one important particular, Leeser anticipated the Revised Version: he arranged the English in paragraphs and not in verses. Since Leeser's day, however, not only have we learned more as to the precise meaning of words, but we have won a closer insight into the idiomatic use of the Hebrew tenses. The American revision, now issued under the auspices of the American Jewish Publication Society, has given us at once a scholarly translation, and one which remains true to the English excellences of the version made in the reign of King James.

Leeser's Bible, therefore, is more or less doomed. It cannot but pass out of general use. But it can never pass out of our esteem and affection. Leeser, though he indignantly repudiated sectarian bias, did not translate the Bible as an exercise in scholar-

ship.   He belonged to those who believed in the
Bible.   Quite naively he tells us in his Preface
(dated September 20, 1853) that he is " an Israelite in faith, in the full sense of the word; he be-
lieves in the Scriptures as they have been handed
down to us; in the truth and authenticity of prophe-
cies and their ultimate literal fulfilment."   Nor did
he think that the age of miracles was past.   He
admitted that there were sources of information
which he had not consulted when preparing his
Bible.   But he had done his best, and felt that he
was therefore working with a hand stronger than
his own.   " I thought, in all due humility, that I
might safely go to the task, confidently relying upon
that superior aid which is never withheld from the
inquirer after truth."   What a combination of
sophistication and simplicity we have here!   In the
mid-nineteenth century such a union of rationalism
and faith was rare; it is growing rarer every day.
We shall soon be thinking of putting Isaac Leeser's
memory in a museum of Jewish antiquities as a
specimen of a lost type.

LANDOR'S " ALFIERI AND SALOMON "

There is only one Jew in Landor's long series of *Imaginary Conversations,* and he was, most probably, an invention of the author's. " Salomon the Florentine Jew," who discourses in Landor's pages with Count Vittorio Alfieri, never existed; at all events he is not identifiable. There is no mention of such a person in Alfieri's autobiography; so Landor's editor—Mr. C. G. Crump—is careful to point out. Still, Landor (1775-1864) spent several years in Florence, and it is possible that he heard of some Jewish worthy whom he used for the purpose of his dialogue.

Landor treats his solitary Jewish character with courtesy. " You are the only man in Florence with whom I would willingly exchange a salutation," says Alfieri at the opening of the conversation. Salomon expresses himself as highly flattered. The actual dialogue is not one of Landor's best, unless it be for its recognition of the sterling quality of the English middle-class. " It is among those who stand between the peerage and the people that there exists a greater mass of virtue and of wisdom

than in the rest of Europe." The historical
Alfieri found himself out of sympathy both with
kings and with the French Revolution which destroyed kingship. It was a happy touch of
Landor's, therefore, to put into Alfieri's mouth the
praise of the class which stood between royalty and
the masses.

But *Alfieri and Salomon* is hardly a successful
work of art. It has neither the romantic beauty of
Landor's *Aesop and Rhodope,* nor the dramatic interest of his *Hannibal and Marcellus.* Naturally,
however, it has some good epigrams. "A poet
can never be an atheist," says Landor's Alfieri. He
calls on God to confound the fools who always
eulogize the least praiseworthy of princes because,
he complains, "the rascals have ruined my physi-
ognomy; I wear an habitual sneer upon my face."
How many a genius has been made similarly dis-
agreeable because he could not suffer fools gladly!
Very true again is Alfieri's paradox that the gravest
people are the wittiest. "Few men have been
graver than Pascal, few have been wittier." Had
Landor's Florentine Salomon been a real Jew, he
could have capped Alfieri's citation of Pascal by
referring to many a Jewish instance, among them
Abraham Ibn Ezra. On the contrary, Salomon

disputes the truth of Alfieri's statement. Landor is fond of national generalizations. " Not a single man of genius hath ever appeared in the whole extent of Austria," he makes Salomon say; while Alfieri asserts that " the Spaniards have no palate, the Italians no scent, the French no ear." Fortunately it did not occur to Landor to sum up the Jews in an epigram. He retained, however, the eighteenth century tolerance, and might have been lenient. The only thing he thoroughly detested was priest-craft, fanaticism. His Salomon confesses that " theology is without attraction " for him, and the saying came from Landor's heart.

There is not much of the Jew in Salomon. He might have been any cultured contemporary of Alfieri. At one point, however, he refuses to hazard a word as to certain clerics, while Alfieri freely judges and condemns them. " The people who would laugh with you, would stone me," says Salomon. Was this really true of the end of the eighteenth century in Italy? I doubt it. Landor is no true guide to the opinions of his age. To continue. Landor's Salomon speaks of Florence as his native city; he knows it and its extraordinary story in every detail; he discusses its men of genius, though he admits: " My ignorance of Greek forbids me to

compare our Dante with Homer." Salomon is
through and through Italian. Perhaps Landor
meant to depict him as a Jew by putting into his
mouth a good anecdote:

A sailor found upon the shore a piece of amber; he carried
it home, and, as he was fond of fiddling, began to rub it across
the strings of his violin. It would not answer. He then broke
some pieces off, boiled them in blacking, and found to his
surprise and disquiet that it gave no fresh lustre to the shoe-
leather. 'What are you about?' cried a messmate. 'Smell
it, man; it is amber.' 'The devil take it,' cried the finder, 'I
fancied it was resin'; and he threw it into the sea. We despise
what we cannot use.

There is one touch in *Alfieri and Salomon* which
makes it look as though the latter were a real personage. Salomon urges Alfieri to ignore his de-
tractors and inferiors, and to be assured that,
though his contemporaries might belittle him, posterity would be more appreciative.

Salomon: All the present race of them, all the creatures in
the world which excite your indignation, will lie in the
grave, while young and old are clapping their hands or
beating their bosoms at your *Bruto Primo*. . . . .
Alfieri: I believe, sir, you were the first in commending my
tragedies.
Salomon: He who first praises a good book becomingly is next
in merit to the author.

That sentence, " you were the first in commending my tragedies," has a genuine ring, it is life-like.
Had Landor any real ground for believing that a
certain Florentine Jew named Salomon or Solomon
was the first to recognize Alfieri's genius for tragedy? It is an interesting fact, if it be a fact. Even
so, it has its curious side. Alfieri (1749-1803) was
a prolific writer of plays, but the best of his tragedies—and his tragedies as a whole were superior
to his comedies—was not his *Brutus*. It is queer
that the Jew should forget which was the best. It
was certainly Alfieri's *Saul,* published in October,
1784. It won more success than any other of his
dramas. His " severe and unadorned manner "
was peculiarly adapted to the rugged simplicity of
the characters which are presented in *Saul*. The
drama deals with the last day of the king, the scene
being laid in the Israelite camp on mount Gilboa.
There are only six characters: Saul, Gionata
(Jonathan), David, Micol, Abner, Achimelech,
with stage armies of " soldati israeliti " and " soldati filistei." Apart from the subtle contrasts between David the warrior and David the minstrel,
the finest thing in the play is the management of
Saul's insanity. Indeed, it has been truly said of
Alfieri: " In the representation of that species of

mental alienation, where the judgment has perished but traces of character still remain, he is peculiarly happy."

Another poet who was in Florence with Landor also chose the subject of Saul for one of his most dramatic efforts. I refer to Robert Browning, who had intellectually much in common with Landor, though his temperament and philosophy of life were quite other. Landor ignored Alfieri's *Saul,* Browning imitated it. Earlier, in 1820, Joseph Ephrathi, no doubt instigated by Alfieri's success, produced a Hebrew drama with Saul as hero. Gutzkow later on wrote a tragedy on the subject. Another who treated of the topic was Byron. He had no likeness to Landor, but was not dissimilar to Alfieri; both were aristocrats, both pretended to cynicism, both were versatile authors, both squanderers of a great opportunity. It is strange that it was left to Alfieri to detect the dramatic possibilities in the tragedy of Saul. Handel's exploitation of the theme was, naturally, musical rather than dramatic. In the new freedom of the English stage we shall, no doubt, soon have plays and to spare on the subject. Landor, as we have seen, makes no use whatever of biblical personages for his dialogues. But English poetry has not done ill with

Saul's memory. Sir Philip Sydney, or one of his age, gave us as beautiful a rendering as we need wish of David's elegy over Saul and Jonathan. What could be more lovely than

> Pleasant they were in life, and fair,
> Nor yet did death their love divide.

or than

> Ah! Jonathan, my brother! lorn
>   And friendless I must look to be!—
> That heart whose woe thou oft hast borne
>   Is sore and stricken now for thee!
> Young bridegroom's love on bridal morn,
>   Oh! it was light to thine for me;
> Thy timeless lot I now must plain,
> Even on thine own high places slain!
> How lowly now the mighty are,
> How still the weapons of the war!

We have got rather far from Landor. Yet I cannot but think that the best thought suggested by his *Alfieri and Salomon* is just Alfieri's *Saul*, to which the parties to the " imaginary conversation " make no allusion.

PART V

PART V

BROWNING'S " BEN KARSHOOK "

Two great literary forces, poets both yet both greater in what they said than in how they said it, expressed their most intimate beliefs on life and destiny under the guise of a Jewish personation. Nathan the Wise, the hero of Lessing's drama, was Lessing, just as Rabbi Ben Ezra, the supposititious soliloquist of Browning's poem was Browning. Lessing, it is certain, had a living model in Moses Mendelssohn. Nathan was drawn from his friend. Had Browning any such model? Yes and no. Many a writer since Furnivall has identified the hero of Browning's poem with Abraham Ibn Ezra. It is probable that the poet had him vaguely in mind. When, however, it is sought—as several have done—to work out the identity in detail, the effort fails. The poet clearly meant to prevent any such error. For in *Holy-Cross Day,* he introduces a Rabbi Ben Ezra as singing a " Song of Death " quite different in tone from the poem in which Rabbi Ben Ezra unfolds his scheme of life.

Browning obviously meant us to infer that Ben Ezra was no one in particular.

Browning's Hebrew knowledge was probably good; like his wife he was apparently able to read the Bible in the original. He also had dipped into curious, out of the way books on Jewish lore. The Rev. Michael Adler cleverly detected that he owed some of the astonishing Hebrew words in his *Jocoseria* to a little read edition of the Itinerary of Benjamin of Tudela. Very bad Hebrew it is, but its author was not Browning but Baratier (see *Jewish Chronicle*, April 25, 1890). On the other hand, Dr. Joseph Jacobs records in the *Jewish Quarterly Review* for April, 1890, an incident which shows that the poet was " shaky " in his use of Hebrew names. One of Browning's most important " Jewish " poems was his *Johanan Hakkadosh,* Johanan the Holy. Dr. Jacobs tells us that the author was about to call this worthy " Hakkadosh Johanan." But " through a common friend I pointed out the error to the poet, and the adjective was put in its proper position." Another misconception of epithets will be noted below.

Similarly with the poem entitled *Ben Karshook's Wisdom.* Who was " Ben Karshook "? I doubt whether the writer could have told. In the

Tauchnitz copy of 1872, as well as in the English edition of 1889, as Mrs. Sutherland Orr points out, the name is spelt " Karshish." Ben Karshook, seems a mere jumble of Ben Hyrkanos. But either way, there was no Rabbi of the name. Elsewhere, Browning employs the name Karshish to designate an Arabian physician. It was one of Browning's foibles, to quote Dr. Jacobs again, to give an impression of recondite learning. Ben Karshook would seem to have been the poet's first attempt at a Jewish, as distinct from a biblical subject. *Holy-Cross Day* was the first to be published; it appeared in 1855. *Rabbi Ben Ezra* came in 1864, *Filippo Baldinucci* in 1876, *Johanan Hakkadosh* (with other Jewish poems) in 1883. This list is not a complete summary, but (if one adds *Abt Vogler*) it includes the most important. *Ben Karshook's Wisdom* was not published until a year later than *Holy-Cross Day,* for it was printed in the *Keepsake* for 1856. But it was written on April 27, 1854 (according to the statement of Berdoe). Browning himself omitted the poem, apparently by accident, from one of his own volumes, where it is included in the table of contents but not in the book. He never reprinted it. The result has been that it has often been reproduced by others for that very reason; and now, though it has been given a place in the Oxford Browning, let it be printed again!

I.

"Would a man 'scape the rod?"
　Rabbi Ben Karshook saith,
"See that he turn to God
　The Day before his death."

"Ay, could a man inquire
　When it shall come?" I say
The Rabbi's eye shoots fire—
　"Then let him turn to-day."

II.

Quoth a young Sadducee:
　"Reader of many rolls,
Is it so certain we
　Have, as they tell us, souls?"

"Son, there is no reply!"
　The Rabbi bit his beard:
"Certain, a soul have *I*—
　We may have none," he sneered.

Thus Karshook, the Hiram's-Hammer,
　The Right-hand Temple-column,
Taught babes in grace their grammar,
　And struck the simple, solemn.

The first part is an apt version of the saying of
Rabbi Eliezer, son of Hyrkanos: " Repent one
day before thy death " (Pirke Abot 2. 15).
Whereon the Talmud (Shabbat 153a) records that
Eliezer's disciples asked Browning's very question,
and received precisely the same answer. The second
group of stanzas introduces us to a young Sadducee who has doubts as to the existence of the
soul. The poet obviously got his information from
Mark, but was a trifle confused as to what he read
there. The Sadducees (Mark 12. 18) denied the
resurrection, and some have supposed their denial
to have extended to the belief in immortality. (See
Dr. Kohler's remarks in the *Jewish Encyclopedia,*
vol. x, p. 631, top of second column.) To Browning this may have seemed equivalent to questioning
the existence of the soul. Assuredly, granted that
there be a soul at all, it must be immortal.

What is the point of calling Karshook " Hiram's
Hammer? " Browning is probably drawing on
Josephus. Hiram, who helped in building the temple, also interchanged difficult problems with Solomon. (*Antiquities,* viii, 5. 3). Hence, Browning
uses the name in relation to these puzzles, so wisely
answered in the poem. It was also Hiram—not
identical with the king of Tyre—who constructed

the two temple columns Jachin and Boaz. Or, as
Dr. Halper has cleverly suggested, the poet may
have had in his mind a confused reminiscence of the
Rabbinic praise of Johanan ben Zaccai, who (in
Berakot 28 b.) is described as *Right-hand Temple-
column, Strong Hammer.* Browning possibly
mixed up the Hebrew *hazak* (strong) with *hiram,*
and so transformed the epithet into "Hiram's
Hammer." If these and similar reminiscences were
passing through Browning's mind, they might well
result in the verse which terminates with the brilliant phrase "struck the simple, solemn." It needs
rare wisdom to make a fool think—or even better,
make him silent.

Dr. Jacobs well summed up our indebtedness to
Browning when he said that "it is not in the
minutiae of Hebrew scholarship that we are to
look for Browning's sympathy with the Jewish
spirit," so markedly shown in his writings. Mr.
Stopford Brooke (*The Poetry of Robert Browning,* 1902, pp. 33-4) puts the case strongly but
truly when he declares that "no English poet, save
perhaps Shakespeare, whose exquisite sympathy
could not leave even Shylock unpitied, had spoken
of the Jew with compassion, knowledge and admiration, till Browning wrote of him. The Jew lay

deep in Browning." The writer of those sentences no doubt would not call Richard Cumberland a poet; his plays were friendly enough to the Jew. But Browning's understanding was more profound than Cumberland's. It is a mistake to say, as a recent critic has said, that " Browning would have us see that the purest religion is of any creed or none." That was perhaps Lessing's view. Browning seems to go further. He saw in Judaism certain elements of absolute truth; therefore he presented those elements through Jewish characters.

K. E. FRANZOS' " JEWS OF BARNOW "

George MacDonald was a novelist of distinction. When an English translation of *Ein Kampf ums Recht* appeared (under the title *For the Right*), MacDonald wrote an introduction. " Not having been asked to do so, I write this preface from admiration of the book." It was a significant fact, he continued, that the generation had produced a man capable of such an ideal as the book represented. It was a work which substituted for the " half wisdom " of the cry " art for art's sake " the whole wisdom of the cry " art for truth's sake." And MacDonald concluded as he began: " I have seldom, if ever, read a work of fiction that moved me with so much admiration." Mr. Gladstone, too, was among the enthusiastic eulogists of the novel.

Its author was Karl Emil Franzos, to whom we owe, besides that masterpiece of his genius, *For the Right* (1887), also the less mature work of his earlier years, *The Jews of Barnow* (1877). He will always be remembered for a saying of his which appeared in his first-published book, a narrative of travel-sketches, *Aus Halb-Asien* (1876) : *Jedes Land hat die Juden die es verdient* (" Every country has the Jew that it deserves "). Macaulay said much the same thing, but less epigrammatically, nearly half a century earlier. It is not a completely satisfactory generalization, but it is an effective counter to the cruel theory that every Jew gets the country he deserves. " It is not the fault of the Polish Jews that they are less civilized than their brethren in the faith in England, Germany, and France." Writing this sentence forty years ago, Franzos used the word " civilized " in a narrow sense. All that it really amounted to was that the conventions of Barnow were not those of Berlin. Franzos makes quite a grim problem out of the Barnow Jewess's revolt against the *Scheitel,* without seeing that in point of fact the revolt was only one, and an early, phase of the new feminist movement which was to spread all over the world.

What were Franzos' qualifications for becoming the historian of a Podolian ghetto? He lived out his boyhood there; and he never lost the Jewish sympathies generated by his early experiences. Years afterwards, when he was at the summit of his renown, the most famous Jewish littérateur of his age, he associated himself heartily at Berlin with the work being done for Israel in Russia. The Barnow of his tales was the Czortkow of his youth. Whether he, therefore, presented a true picture is not so certain. He himself was convinced that, though he strove to give poetic value to the scenes, he none the less depicted the scenes accurately. " I have never permitted my love of the beautiful to lead me into the sin of falsifying the facts and conditions of life, and am confident that I have described this strange and outlandish mode of existence precisely as it appeared to me." Franzos' claim that he drew a sincere picture cannot be disputed, but a sincere picture is not necessarily an accurate one. Things may not " appear " to one truly. How stands it with Franzos?

The Barnow of the tale is a gloomy little town, and the houses of its ghetto small and dirty. Yet it boasts the great white mansion of its millionaire; it has its real spring days when the air is deliciously soft and warm. And it knows how to keep the Sabbath, how to welcome the bride with an emotion which stirs its spirit to the very depths. But all the passion is expended on the adoration of the Divinity. " The same race whose genius gave birth to the Song of Songs—the eternal hymn of love—and to whom the world owes the story of

Ruth, the most beautiful idyl of womanhood ever known—has now, after a thousand years of the night of oppression and wandering, learned to look on marriage as a mere matter of business, by which to secure some pecuniary advantage, and as a means of preventing the chosen of the Lord from dying off the face of the earth." The author grows more and more indignant as he writes: "These men know not what they do—they have no suspicion of the sin of which they are guilty in thus acting."

This, for Franzos, was the tragedy of Barnow. It is the theme of several of his tales. Sometimes it is the boy, sometimes the girl, who rides a-tilt against the paternal choice of a mate. The father selects for his son or daughter the most pious and wealthy partner available. They will not know each other, but what of that? They will have plenty of time to make acquaintance after marriage. One Barnow father thus defends the system: "We don't look upon the chicken as wiser than the hen. And, thank God, we know nothing of love and all that kind of nonsense. We consider that two things are alone requisite when arranging a marriage, and these are health and wealth. The bride and bridegroom in this case possess both." Franzos obviously regards this justification as one of the

" outlandish " features of Barnow's manners. But were he alive to-day, he would recognize that Moses Freudenthal, the Barnow father who thus argues, was anticipating the latest formula of Eugenics! The novelist, however, remorselessly sees only the tragedy and not the amenities of the system. From the side of the man, in the story *Nameless Graves,* Franzos put it thus: " As a general rule, the long-haired Jewish youth never even thinks of any girl until his father tells him that he has chosen a wife for him. He sometimes sees his bride for the first time at betrothal, but in a great many cases he does not see her until his marriage-day; and then, whether she pleases him or not, he makes up his mind to get used to her, and generally succeeds." But the Barnow young men turn and look at Lea as she walks down the street—" a thing hitherto unknown." Even in the *Klaus,* when " quiet, dreamy, and very dirty Talmudists bent over their heavy folios, her name was sometimes mentioned, followed by many a deep sigh." A revolution in male manners, undoubtedly.

On the other side, things are even worse in Barnow. If the men actually think of choosing for themselves, the women go and do likewise. And with fatal results. Half educated, feasting

on surreptitious and precocious courses of the
works of Paul de Kock, fascinated by Christian
lovers, the girls of Barnow go through agitating
experiences, sometimes heading for the rocks, always wrecking the harmony of the home. Esther
and Chane differ only in externals; the one openly
defies Mrs. Grundy, the other, in appearance only,
obeys her. But both are led by passion to kick
over the traces; both are treated by Franzos as vic-
tims of the loveless marriage system. Esterka
Regina makes renunciation, but her last act was to
write to the lover—a Jew this time—whom she
had renounced, practically to confess to him that
her marriage had been a failure. She had chosen
the course mapped out by her parents, not from
motives of obedience, but because her ignorant
bringing-up had unfitted her for the position she
would have had to occupy had she followed the dictates of her heart.

I have hinted above my doubts whether Franzos
drew for us a correct picture of Barnow conditions.
Amid all the realistic touches, here and there one
comes across evidence of defective vision. He
painted Barnow as he saw it, but he did not see it
as it was. His father was district physician, a real
friend of his fellow-Jews, but not living their life.

The son saw Galician Jewish life from an aloof point of view. It is significant that in one of his tales he confuses the Friday eve with the Saturday night prayers. It is a slip with no serious consequences, but it does reveal the limitations of Franzos' knowledge. None of his tragic heroines strikes so convincing a note as does, for instance, Bernstein's graciously pathetic Voegele. Bernstein ceased to be a Jew, while Franzos remained faithful. Spiritual fidelity, however, does not necessarily carry with it realistic artistry.

HERZBERG'S " FAMILY PAPERS "

Wilhelm Herzberg was a victim to the world's sensitiveness. And a queer sensitiveness it is! You may abuse a man as much as you like, and as unfairly as you like, while he is alive. But you must not speak harsh, even if they be true, things of him when he is recently dead. *De mortuis nil nisi bonum!* After a decent interval, criticism may resume operations. But for the hour you may only say soft things of the departed.

Far be from me to deny that there is an amiable and humane side to this convention. For my part, I prefer to moderate my judgments while the man is still alive. I do not admire over much those who bespatter another with abuse in his lifetime, and with flattery in the moment of his death. But the world thinks differently. Herzberg sinned against this convention; he wrote severely, even bitterly, and also unjustly, of an Anglo-Jewish worthy soon after the interment of the latter. And so he lost his friends, and was ostracized here for the rest of his own life. He resigned his post as Director of the Jerusalem Orphanage—though probably for other reasons. He died in Brussels in 1898.

The incident alluded to in these preceding lines was typical of the man's nature. He was not easy to get on with. He was not so much quarrelsome as aggressive. Witty, keen-minded, he was above all a man of impulsive emotions. He never defended a cause; he always attacked its opponents. If his fortress were besieged, he answered with a sortie; he could not fight behind the walls. And this is true of the wonderful book which, under the pen-name of " Gustav Meinhardt," he first published in Hamburg in 1868, calling it *Jüdische Familienpapiere*. It is the most brilliant vindication of Judaism published in the nineteenth century. But it is an attack on rival systems more than a mere apology for his own religion. The author throughout is plaintiff rather than defendant.

The book consists of a series of letters written from Germany to England. The author of the letters is a youth, Samuel; the recipient of them is an Englishman of means, Samuel's adoptive father. A Jew by birth, Samuel has been brought up in England as a Christian by the kind-hearted aristocrat, who found the child destitute after the death of his real father, a poor hawker. And now he is sent home to his Jewish relatives on a mission— he is to convert them to his new faith. The letters describe Samuel's arrival in the abode of his uncle, Rabbi Nathan, and with exquisite charm unfold the gradual reversion of Samuel to his ancestral allegiance. This part of the book is certainly constructive enough. Samuel is overwhelmed with his discoveries. He is fascinated by Rabbi Nathan, and also by his cousin, Rachel. I think it would be difficult to find in literature a more beautiful description of Jewish home-life than Herzberg presents. No wonder that in the end the would-be converter becomes the converted.

The great part of the argument, however, is occupied less with showing the success of Judaism, than the failure of Christianity. Herzberg speaks out; there is no hesitation, no reserve. He never loses his courteous manner, but this formal suavity does not mitigate the truculence of the statements he makes, the severity of the arguments he uses. He is one-sided in that he sets the Church's failure against the Synagogue's success, and does not attempt to balance against each other the successes of each and the failures of each. But he is confessedly an advocate and not a judge. It is this that makes his book so valuable. It is an outspoken criticism of modern culture by a well-equipped mind. For to Herzberg, naturally and rightly enough, the

Church is typical of Western civilization. Attacking the former, he is assailing the latter, denying the validity of Western—or rather—Germanic, ideals, and disputing their permanent worth.

Before pointing out in a sentence the significance of this attitude for the present condition of Jewish thought, one or two other things must be said about the book. There were three German editions in the author's lifetime, the third appearing in Zurich in 1893. Why was the third issue made in Switzerland and not in Hamburg? In the circular announcing it, Cæsar Schmidt made a remarkable statement. The author had been urged by his friend to soften some parts of it. He refused. Anti-Semitism made the book, in its unaltered shape, the more necessary; but it also made it desirable to issue it in " free Switzerland." The author would have bettered the book in one sense, had he yielded to his friend's counsel. Its historical surveys are not unassailable, and its logic is not always perfect. Yet to have modified its polemical tone would have been to destroy its efficacy. Moreover, Herzberg's friends can have known little of him if they imagined that he would alter even a comma to please them! I met him several times before 1893, and I could have told them that they were wasting their time in giving him advice. He always went his own way; and he would have been the last to complain because that way was a rugged one.

The author had this satisfaction: his work was enthusiastically admired by a notable circle of readers. Graetz had a high opinion of it. David Kaufmann, a lad of sixteen at the time of its first appearance, was its ardent eulogist; to him the third edition is inscribed. "You will find your erstwhile darling unchanged; for to change it would be to mangle it"—so writes Herzberg to Kaufmann. One would not talk of changing it now, for one does not mutilate classics.

Kaufmann, young as he was in 1868, was already a student of the Breslau Seminary. Let another student of the same institution tell us of the impression the *Family Papers* made there. Dr. F. de Sola Mendes writes that "he was yet studying at the Breslau Theological Seminary when the book was first brought under his notice by a fellow-student, one of its most enthusiastic admirers. A large number of copies were at once procured and read with avidity by our comrades. It is impossible to describe the applause the book called forth; never had we read so glowing and so powerful a vindication of pure Judaism. We were rejoiced that the country which produced an Eisenmenger, a Wagenseil, Schudt, Pfefferkorn *et hoc genus omne,* should have yielded in our day, too, so triumphant a Defender of the Faith. Our venerable Director, Dr. Frankel, was as enthusiastic as any of his young disciples in its praise." The writer of the lines just quoted determined to render the book into English. " The work of translation was commenced and carried on in leisure intervals for the next few years. In January, 1874, in conjunction with Mr. A. Herzberg, then of London, brother of the author, a prospectus was issued in England, proposing the publication of the work by subscription. The project was heartily indorsed by the Chief Rabbi and Dr. H. Adler, the latter of whom kindly made valuable suggestions as to omissions and alterations proper in a version to come before average English readers." One wonders what the author would have said to such " omissions and alterations." But the matter was not taken up by the Anglo-Jewish public, and Dr. Mendes eventually issued his excellent translation in New York (1875), under the auspices of that American Jewish Publication Society which preceded the present organization bearing the same name.

There must clearly be much significance in a work which has from time to time aroused so much feeling. As a boy, I read it with mingled delight and consternation. Even then, unconsciously, I must have had a premonition of its inner meaning. I promised above to sum up its import in a sentence, and I can do it. *Herzberg stands in line with Ahad ha-'Am.* The former does not give a Zionist turn to his exposition, nor does he speak of a *Hebrew* culture. But he is practically at the same standpoint. Civilization for the Jew must be expressed in Jewish terms. That is the real moral of Herzberg's work. Now, as of old, I face such an ideal with delight, but also with consternation. It gives us back much we were in danger of losing, but it tends to take away from us much that we had gained.

LONGFELLOW'S "JUDAS MACCABÆUS"

Whenever Handel's melody falls on one's ears, it is impossible to miss the musical beauty of the chorus:

> See the conquering hero comes,
> Sound the trumpets, beat the drums.

But the words make one shudder. They are so turgid, so inappropriate. Judas Maccabæus, of all men, to strut forth to such a welcome—he, who belonged to the first of those who declared:

> Not unto us, O Lord, not unto us,
> But unto Thy name give glory!

Tennyson speaks of "perfect music set unto noble words." Handel's music may be as perfect as art is capable of, but his librettist betrayed him by supplying words far from noble. They would better have suited Antiochus than Judas. In fact, Handel originally wrote the melody for Joshua who would have approved them as little as the Maccabee.

We still have to wait for a really great drama written round Judas Maccabæus as hero. The most has therefore been made of Longfellow's attempt, which was turned into Yiddish by Belinson (1882) and into Hebrew by Massel (1900). Judas is not an easy character to draw. He was truculent enough, yet there must have been a fascinating sweetness in him. The key-note is struck in a phrase supplied by the First Book of the Maccabees. He and his brethren " fought with gladness the battle of Israel." The *joyousness* of duty is a touch which marks off the Maccabees from the Puritans, and which, developed in Israel's after-history, helped to form the Jewish character. Longfellow, who wrote his *Judas Maccabæus* in 1872, when he had passed the zenith of his powers, misses the point altogether.

Yet he realizes other aspects of his hero's disposition. He partly, though not completely, shares Handel's mistake of turning Judas into a braggart. But he atones by presenting very fully the *sentimentality* of the Maccabee. To dub a warrior sentimental may seem contradictory, but the finest soldiers have been just the most sentimental. In Judas, sentimentality shows itself chiefly in his seizing upon associations aroused by local scenery. Wherever he happens to be—so the historians of his age inform us—he recalls past incidents which occurred there. Here, again, we have in Judas a quality which afterwards became a deep-seated characteristic of the Jew, his romanticism. Long-fellow was himself a romantic as well as a Puritan, and perfectly presents this side of Judas's disposition. Thus at Beth-horon Judas recalls how, on the same battlefield, Joshua,

> The great captain of the hosts of God,
> A slave brought up in the brick-fields of Egypt,
> O'ercame the Amorites. There was no day
> Like that, before or after it, nor shall be.
> The sun stood still; the hammers of the hail
> Beat on their harness; and the captains set
> Their weary feet upon the necks of kings,
> As I will upon thine, Antiochus,
> Thou man of blood!—Behold, the rising sun
> Strikes on the golden letters of my banner,
> *Be Elohim Yehovah!* Who is like
> To thee, O Lord among the gods?—Alas!
> I am not Joshua, I cannot say,
> " Sun, stand thou still on Gibeon, and thou Moon
> In Ajalon!" Nor am I one who wastes
> The fateful time in useless lamentation:
> But one who bears his life upon his hand
> To lose it or to save it, as may best
> Serve the designs of Him who giveth life.

The " nor shall be " which closes the fourth line of this quotation is a false note. The Maccabee

did expect to repeat Joshua's glory; that expecta-
tion of recurrent providences was the basis of
Israel's belief in Providence.   Again, even though
in his day Hebrew had given way to Aramaic as
the national speech (let some of our Hebrew
zealots remember that Judas Maccabæus did *not*
talk in Hebrew!), none the less Judas would hardly
have been guilty of the error to begin a Hebrew
sentence in the middle.   Yet Longfellow repeats
this curious slip later on, making Judas rush to battle, shouting *Be Elohim Yehovah!* as though
" Among the gods, O Lord " (for that is what the
Hebrew words mean) could possibly be a war-cry.
No doubt he knew that in one theory the name
Maccabee is explained as the initials of the Hebrew
text " Who is like unto Thee among the mighty
(or the gods), O Lord."   But it was a queer confusion that made him employ the second half of
the verse as a signal, and to substitute *elohim* for
the *elim* of the Song of Moses (Exod. 15. 11).   I
say nothing of his putting into Judas' mouth the
monstrosity *Yehovah*—a misspelling (more common in the form *Jehovah*) which was invented
about the year 1520 by the reformers.   As is well
known, the misspelling arose by reading the *vowels*
of *adonai* (Lord), as the Name was quite early

read, with the consonants of the Name as written in the Hebrew text.

In another aspect Longfellow is perhaps unfairly kind to Judas. Henry V, as Shakespeare drew him, was something of a braggadocio. But the dramatist might almost have been thinking of Judas when he makes his Henry exclaim before Agincourt: " I pray thee, wish not one man more." Judas, too, knew that much of the glory of victory depended upon the success of the few over the many, " the fewer men the greater share of honour." Judas, unlike Henry, would have meant the more signal would be the revelation of God's power, if the human means by which the battle was won were weaker. On the other hand, the Books of the Maccabees do not, so far as one's memory goes, indicate that Judas, any more than Henry, was chivalrous in the narrower sense. The Jewish exemplar of the chivalrous warrior is David not Judas. Longfellow, however, presents Judas as the chivalrous knight. One hesitates what to think of the third scene in Act III of Longfellow's play. In " mysterious guise," Nicanor enters the Jewish camp, a herald " unheralded," gliding " like a serpent silently " into the very presence of Judas. Nicanor discovers himself.

Judas: Thou art indeed Nicanor. I salute thee.
  What brings thee hither to this hostile camp
  Thus unattended?

Nicanor: Confidence in thee.
  Thou hast the noble virtues of thy race,
  Without the failings that attend those virtues.
  Thou can'st be strong, and yet not tyrannous,
  Can'st righteous be and not intolerant.
  Let there be peace between us.

Judas: What is peace?
  Is it to bow in silence to our victors?
  Is it to see our cities sacked and pillaged?
  Our people slain, or sold as slaves, or fleeing
  At night-time by the blaze of burning towns;
  Jerusalem laid waste; the Holy Temple
  Polluted with strange gods? Are these things peace?

This is cleverly conceived. Nicanor's degrading compliments as well as his false offer of peace are rejected with due scorn. Longfellow probably got the idea for this scene from the story told of Mattathias, to whom the Syrian envoys made overtures, which the dour father of the Maccabee knew how to treat. But what one doubts is whether Nicanor would have trusted himself to the Maccabean camp. The scene ends:

Judas: Go to thy tents.
Nicanor: Shall it be war or peace?

Judas: War, war, and only war. Go to thy tents
    That shall be scattered, as by you were scattered
    The torn and trampled pages of the Law,
    Blown through the windy streets.
Nicanor: Farewell, brave foe!
Judas: Ho, there, my captains! Have safe conduct given
    Unto Nicanor's herald through the camp,
    And come yourselves to me.—Farewell, Nicanor!

One wonders whether such an end to such a scene were possible? Still, if David would have acted thus generously, why not Judas? We must allow for the insight of genius. Longfellow may have understood the story more truly than his critic. If to the valor, the recklessness of self, the romanticism, the all-pervading joyousness of Judas, we may add the trait of generosity, then is he indeed among the noblest models of chivalry which history can show.

ARTOM'S SERMONS

When, in February, 1873, Haham Artom was pressed to publish a selection of his Sermons, he consented, but with reluctance. For, said he, " I am fully aware of the difficulty of speaking and writing in a language which is not my own . . . . a language which, some years ago, was unknown to me." Artom never lost his Italian accent, and the slight survival of his native idiom added grace to his English orations. He was an attractive figure in the pulpit; and as effective as attractive.

He died in 1879. Having frequently heard him preach, having, indeed, been present when many of these very addresses were first given, I have again, after more than forty years, turned to the printed volume. Is any of the fire left? Has all the charm evaporated? His commanding presence, his beautiful voice, his dramatic gestures, his extempore delivery of carefully prepared impromptus—were these mannerisms answerable for the whole of Artom's power, or was there something forceful and persuasive in the matter? In a word, do the speeches survive the speaker?

Let us remember, first and last, that Artom was an artist. He not only wrote verses, but he composed music; some of his melodies are still sung in the Sephardic synagogues. He was also an artist in prose. This gift sometimes led him astray. The faults of the speaker certainly remain in the speeches. The passages which sounded grotesque in the hearing, strike one in the reading as more grotesque still. For instance, in his sermon (November 7, 1874) against Cremation, he describes in lurid detail the scene at the burning of the body, and then he proceeds: " A sad and repeated crackling is soon heard; the combustion is going on rapidly. But to my ears that crackling seems to be the complaint of the dead person for being treated with such cruelty and disrespect."

This is sentimentalism at its falsest. Obviously, such faults of the orator endure. Have his merits the same lasting quality? The question may be confidently answered in the affirmative.

He showed true artistry in structure. A preacher must be a builder. He has to construct a work of art. Not merely in the sense of form, but also and chiefly in substance. Judaism is the home beautiful; it fascinates the eye, but it also provides rooms for living. Artom entertained, and he also fed his guests. Out of his sermons you could easily piece together a fine edifice of Judaism. Many of its greatest truths are there, presented very solidly, and for all his decorative art very simply. Artom was not a thinker, he was a believer. Yet, though he never felt a doubt, he always realized that there were people who differed from him. He was thus frequently controversial; he had in mind some other opinions which he was determined to combat. This method impelled him to present religion in relation to the realities of his day. No preacher can be effective, unless he does so; no preacher's words endure for other times, unless they are first vital for his own.

In another respect, Artom's method justified itself. I refer to his use of rabbinic quotations. He seldom quoted anything else. Here we have, in part, a mere trick, a mechanical device, artificial rather than artistic. Every sermon is headed by two texts, the one scriptural, the other rabbinic. In those olden Jewish homilies called, from their opening formula, *Yelammedenu* a similar plan was followed, but the rabbinic passage was legal, involving some problem of Halakah or practical laws. Artom's citations are always homiletical, and rarely add to the effect of the biblical text. Mechanical, too, is the division of each address into a Prologue, followed by three parts, ending with an Epilogue culminating in a prayer. The whole congregation almost invariably rose at the close of the Haham's sermons, to join in these prayers, spoken with genuine but never unctious fervor. Such severe divisions of the sermon were long *de rigueur* on the continent. Nowadays, in the reaction against these fetters, sermons tend to lose *form* altogether. But where Artom showed himself a master was in his use of Midrash in the body of his addresses. He had nothing like the theological profundity of Jellinek, who employed Midrash to enforce fundamental ideas with subtlety. Nor had he Jellinek's power of " holding the Midrash in chemical solution." As Mr. Singer— a greater preacher far than Artom— said in his Memoir of Jellinek, midrashic quotations in a sermon are as a rule " stuck clumsily into the discourse, and leave upon the palate the flavour of undissolved spice or sugar in an ill-prepared Sabbath or Festival dish. In Jellinek the assimilation is perfect. It is the bone of his bone and flesh of his flesh. Whether the Midrash or the preacher's theme came first, which went the longer way to meet the other, is often as uncertain to determine as the question, in the case of some of the finest songs, whether the music suggested the words, or the words the music."

300

Artom did not reach the perfection of Jellinek, but he never sank to the level of the botcher. What he aimed at he succeeded in attaining. If his rabbinic quotations at the beginning of a discourse were perfunctory, those which he made in the body of the discourse were invariably to the point; they always interpreted. He did not merge Midrash into his own personality as Jellinek did. But he employed it as a certain type of painter does the accessories to a picture, to add color, to relieve the severity of the main idea, to suggest outwardly that which he is not quite able to express inwardly. Hence he usually quoted obvious Midrashim, and used them in an obvious sense. He showed his wisdom in this. If a painter puts in a camel to help me to perceive that he is representing a desert, he must be very careful to make his camel recognizable. It will not do to give me a symbolical " Ship of the Desert," it must be a camel, palpable and conventional. Within his limitations, he shows himself the better artist the less he tries to make his accessories bizarre or even original.

I trust that no one will suspect me of a desire to " damn with faint praise." On the contrary, starting with the unquestionable fact that the living Artom was a great preacher, my intention was to indicate what we have to keep in mind if we would admire his printed addresses as they deserve. If we know what to expect from them we shall find it. Take the following paragraph:

"Our sages said that 'a precious jewel hung around the neck of Abraham.' It was not a talisman, an amulet, supposed by the superstitious to keep away the consequence of envy, of evil eye; the jewel was the knowledge of the Lord, of the one God, of the Omnipotent Being, that knowledge which Abraham disseminated among men; it was the spiritual jewel which ought to be treasured in the heart of every good man, of every true Israelite. We have inherited that Jewel, we have it still. Oh, let us wear it with pride, for it is the noblest decoration."

There are a hundred such passages in Artom's volume. They got home when the orator pronounced them, and they get home still when calmly read as literature. It is perhaps curious that a preacher who in his day was admired for his brilliance, should endure less for the sparkle than for the substance of what he said. That is, however, the common fate of orators. Happy they, if their utterances have worth after the personality behind them has passed away.

SALKINSON'S " OTHELLO "

One of the first writers to combat, on the continent of Europe, Voltaire's depreciation of Shakespeare was Lessing. But his eulogy was dated 1759. A year earlier (1758) Moses Mendelssohn, in his essay on the Sublime, had anticipated Lessing's judgment. But his influence did not lead the new-Hebrew school to translate Shakespeare. It was not till near the middle of the nineteenth century that we find Hebrew translations even of such famous soliloquies as Hamlet's " To be or not to be." In 1842 Fabius Mieses and in 1856 N. P. Krassensohn rendered the passage. Both, however, were dependent on Mendelssohn, translating his German rendering. Others, at the same period, turned a few passages, including one of Richard II's monologues, from German versions into Hebrew.

" To-day we exact our revenge from the English! They took our Bible and made it their own. We, in return, have captured their Shakespeare. Is it not a sweet revenge? " With these words Smolenskin opened his introduction to Salkinson's Hebrew translation of *Othello*.

303

It is not easy to explain how it happened that we had to wait till 1874 for the first Hebrew adaptation of a Shakespearean drama. In fact, with the exception of Salkinson's *Romeo and Juliet* (1878), S. L. Gordon's *King Lear* (1899), and Isaac Barb's *Macbeth* (1883), I know of no Hebrew version of plays by the author of *Hamlet,* which latter drama so far as I have observed, has not even been printed in Yiddish. (Dr. Halper, however, informs me that *Hamlet* was translated into Hebrew by H. J. Bornstein, and that his version appeared in the pages of Ha-Zefirah somewhere about 1900). *Julius Cæsar* appeared in Yiddish in 1886. *King Lear* has also been printed in the same language, and the *Merchant of Venice* received the same honor, at the hand of Basil Dahl, in New York, in 1899. I use the words *" printed* in Yiddish " advisedly, because there are extant in manuscript acting versions of other plays used by Yiddish companies. Of course, select passages from Shakespeare have often been rendered into Hebrew, as, for instance, in that curious publication *Young's Israelitish Gleaner and Biblical Repository,* Edinburgh, 1855 (pp. 24, 16). The lack of Hebrew translations may be explained by two considerations. The *Merchant of Venice,* despite its sympathetic treatment of some aspects of Shylock's character, dealt so deadly a blow at the Jews, that there could be no enthusiasm with regard to the other works. But more operative was another fact. The available Hebraists for the most part were ignorant of English. The *Macbeth* mentioned above was translated not from the original, but from Schiller's German.

There is a further consideration (for after all Schlegel's fine German version was at hand for those who knew no English). Drama in Hebrew, whether original or translated, has always been spasmodic. Drama needs an audience. Until the Hebrew revival become wider spread, there can never be a sufficiently popular demand for the presentation of Hebrew plays to encourage or cultivate the composition of them. It will no doubt be otherwise in the new Palestine. Indeed we already read of plans, instituted by M. James Rothschild, to organize a Hebrew Drama in Judæa.

Isaac Edward (Eliezer) Salkinson, however, knew English well. He was also gifted with a fine command of Hebrew, which he wrote not only fluently, but in real poetic style. He was born in Wilna, being perhaps the son of Solomon Salkind, himself a writer of meritorious Hebrew verse

(*Jewish Encyclopedia,* vol. x, p. 651). Unfortunately, a knowledge of Hebrew does not of itself suffice to keep a Jew within the pale of the Synagogue. " As a youth, Salkinson set out for America with the intention of entering a rabbinical seminary there; but while in London he was met by agents of the London Missionary Society, and was persuaded to forsake Judaism." The Synagogue lost in him one of the most accomplished Hebraists of modern times.

But though he was lost, his work—or some of it—remains to us, and we ought not to let it go. Nahum Slousch makes an admirable remark on the subject in his *Renascence of Hebrew Literature* (p. 245). Salkinson's first great translation was not of Shakespeare, but of Milton. In 1871 appeared a delightful Hebrew version of *Paradise Lost.* It was a masterly rendering, attaining almost to absolute perfection. Take Salkinson's title. He called it *Vayegaresh et ha-adam* (" So He drove out the man," from Genesis 3. 24). How much apter it is for *Paradise Lost* than Meir Letteris *Ben Abuyah* for Goethe's *Faust.* Salkinson's version is genuine Milton. " It was a sign of the times," says Slousch of Salkinson's rendering of an epic so Christian in character, " that this work of art was enjoyed and appreciated by the educated Hebrew public in due accordance with its literary merits." It was, in brief, an indication that Jewish readers of Hebrew were discriminating between form and substance. Many who are as old as I am can recall a similar change in feeling with regard to pictures. To go through a great Art Gallery was a tax on one's forbearance. Madonnas at every turn offended the Jewish consciousness. Now, however, a large number find it quite easy to admire an artist's talent irrespective of the subject. Yet Josef Israels never painted a Madonna, though he was strongly urged to do so by eminent admirers of his genius.

In the case of Shakespeare's *Othello* no such problem as this arises. In finding a Hebrew title for it, Salkinson did not seek for any paraphrase. He just searched for a Hebrew name which would sound like " Othello," and he found it in the biblical " Ithiel," which may signify " God is with me." " Ithiel " would thus mean much the same as " Immanuel " (" God is with us "). It cannot be asserted that " Ithiel " fails to correspond in sense with " Othello," for the simple reason that no one seems to know what " Othello " means; Ruskin suggested the sense *careful*. On the other hand,

" Iago " is probably a variant of " Jacob "; Salkinson calls him Doeg: there is some similarity in character, as in a name, between the false Doeg and the wily Iago. The other names call for little comment. Desdemona becomes Asenath, not a happy choice, for while Desdemona apparently means the " unfortunate," Asenath is probably the Egyptian for the " Favorite of Neith." Cassio is Cesed—a mere assonance. On the other hand, the Clown is *Lez* (the scoffer); this is a reproduction of meaning, not of sound. After all, not the names, but the play is the thing. Salkinson certainly gives us the play. His Hebrew is the real Shakespeare. Often have I found in difficult passages of the English that the Hebrew is a useful help to the understanding of the original. Sometimes a hasty reader of Salkinson may think that the translator erred, as in his rendering of Othello's last pathetic speech:

> Speak of me as I am; nothing extenuate,
> Nor set down aught in malice: then must you speak
> Of one that loved not wisely but too well;
> Of one not easily jealous, but being wrought,
> Perplex'd in the extreme; of one whose hand,
> Like the base *Indian,* threw a pearl away
> Richer than all his tribe.

Salkinson turns these last two lines into:

> Like the despicable *Jew,* who threw a pearl away
> Richer than all the wealth of Israel.

It is no mistake. There is good authority for reading *Judean* in the English text in place of *Indian.* The most plausible suggestion is Theobald's, that Shakespeare was referring to Herod and Mariamne. The whole of this speech is a triumph of literalness combined with beauty of phraseology. If Salkinson had only written this one page he would be famous among modern Hebraists.

Othello was done into Hebrew at the suggestion of Perez Smolenskin, himself, of course, a noted pioneer of the new-Hebrew school. Smolenskin was delighted with Salkinson's performance. " See," he cried, " how Shakespeare lends himself to Hebrew. While so many are translating into Hebrew works utterly foreign to the Hebraic spirit, here we have one who has chosen a poem which lies near to that spirit." There is much truth in this contention. English does very readily lend itself to translation into Hebrew, just as is the case when the relation is reversed. No version of the Hebrew Bible, not even Luther's, has ever approached the English in its fidelity to the soul of the original. But Smolenskin goes on to use another argument, which is somewhat amusing. He draws a picture of the Jewry of his day, and then exclaims: Lo! here are the very conditions presented to us in *Othello*. And he bids his contemporaries to draw a moral from the play, to regulate their conduct by it. I should hardly justify an appreciation of *Othello* on moral grounds. It is a great psychological drama, and it also touches the pinnacle of romanticism. But a moral? Smolenskin seems to have found in it a warning to men to treat women better. Certainly one would prefer that our Othellos should be a little milder towards their Desdemonas in real life.

All this is off the point. Salkinson's merit lay just in his power to take a work of art, pass it through the crucible of translation, and then bring out the result as a work of art still. Translators are not always traitors. I have said nothing about Salkinson's *Romeo and Juliet,* because his *Othello* came first. But in the former he reveals the same qualities. I do not know whom I would place above Salkinson in the list of the best translators into Hebrew.

310

"LIFE THOUGHTS" OF MICHAEL HENRY

Michael Henry died in 1875. In the following year a volume of his *Life Thoughts* was issued. There are twenty-one chapters, all of them reprinted from the series of "Sabbath Readings," issued by the Jewish Association for the Diffusion of Religious Knowledge. The Association, which, I take pride to remember, was founded by my father, was afterwards transformed into the Jewish Religious Education Board. The Association took a broader view of its function than does the Board; at all events, the discontinuance of the tracts called Sabbath Readings was a deplorable but not irremediable error.

The *Life Thoughts* of Michael Henry corresponded to his life. Their cheery optimism was part of the man's self. Their philosophy is not profound, their learning is not conspicuous. But they make for happiness. Michael Henry was happy when he made others happy, and he succeeded in his genial ambition. He was only forty-five when his career ended, but he had crowded in

311

that short space many a momentous service, especially to the boys and girls whom he loved as though an elder brother to all of them. It was the Jewish boys and girls who in 1876 presented the first " Michael Henry " to the Royal National Lifeboat Institution. The boat was twice replaced by other " Michael Henrys," and the three boats named after " the scholars' friend " have saved 136 lives. From time to time appeals are certain to be made for funds to enable further " Michael Henrys " to be launched.

If to bring joy into a life is to save it, then the man Michael Henry saved more lives than all the boats named, or to be named, after him. I have already spoken of his geniality. A word must be added as to his piety. Religion to him was the spring of conduct. Here, again, his optimism reigned supreme. Judaism was the road to good, on earth and in heaven. In his *Gossip with Boys* he exclaims : " You may be very good Jews and yet very happy ones. Virtue and enjoyment are not incompatible. It is not unmanly to be good. Your right arm will fling a cricket-ball none the less deftly because your left arm has worn the *tephillin* an hour before you went into the play-ground. Your heart will beat none the less bravely, because it throbs against the four-cornered band of the *tsitsith.*" These sentences crystallize Michael Henry's appeal to the young for manliness and confidence.

Virtue is happiness, duty is manliness —these axioms sum up his creed. " The smile of hope " he perceives in the " Psalms of David." He hears music, he smells perfume in " Home worship." He tells the " Barmitzvah " that " by imitation of good, great and true men, the work shall be done and triumph crown the toil." The law and the life which " Moses " proclaimed and led are " both glorious and gracious gifts of heaven to earth." " Happy we," he cries in his *Elijah,* " if when we pass away we leave behind us, like Elijah, a twofold portion of the spirit which those whom we love have every reason to desire of us ! " From " Josiah " young and old may learn that " the most manly king of Judah was also the most religious "; so, too, the character of " Nehemiah " was a " combination of manliness and holiness." " Moses Mendelssohn " enables us to learn to be " good and happy," and, adds Michael Henry, " it is refreshing to turn from the troubled stories of kings, warriors, and statesmen, to the record of this calm, pure life, in which, as in the religion he followed, peace, love and wisdom are harmoniously combined." In his *Message of Love* (Leviticus 19. 18), he quotes with a croon of delight the poet's thought *Seid umschlungen, Millionen* (" Millions! be locked in one embrace ").

In his paper on " Peace " he enumerates the practical means by which that end may be advanced, and he continues: " Thus we can promote peace *outwardly* in the world, and by that effort pomote peace *inwardly* in our hearts; we can spread around us a peace of earth like a sun-picture of the spiritual peace we ask from Heaven for ourselves." Then, in his paper on " Heaven upon Earth," he argues that Judaism does not tell us " to strive against the very nature of our being." There is a not very thickly veiled controversialism in the sentences that follow: " We need not turn the left cheek when stricken on the right, nor impoverish ourselves to enrich the poor, nor let the guilty go free because we are not righteous enough to punish, nor leave the holy charms of family delights to follow the standard of fanatical self-denial. But what we have to do is this: True to the teachings of our faith, we have to take our nature as it is; with all its aims, its passions, its impulses; and, beating the evil from it as the thresher

314

strikes the chaff from the grain, or the smelter frees the dross from the gold, we must shape and trim the pure material into its best form, and work it to its best purpose, drawing from it all that it has of good; giving to all its strength an upward tendency." But Michael Henry is not at his best when he is arguing. We enjoy him in his unreasoning but fascinating optimism, as when, in *The Everlasting Light,* after describing the troubles and clouds of life and destiny, he comfortably assures us: " Have faith, and it all seems easy." We see the real Michael Henry in the three stories or rather parables with which the volume ends, " How we Spoilt our Holiday," the " Schoolboy and the Angel," and the " Everlasting Rose." These three chapters at least would bear reprinting. They express Michael Henry in his most charming aspects of sincerity, clean-heartedness, and unconquerable belief in the ideal.

But there is one chapter missing from the *Life Thoughts* of Michael Henry. It is a strange omission. No man ever excelled the subject of this article in his power to harmonize his religion with his life. Michael Henry as pietist, as lover of children, as editor of the *Jewish Chronicle* (from 1868), as agent for patents—under all these aspects the man was one and the same. His *Life Thoughts* are a torso, unless we draw on his writings as a mechanician. To restrict the selection to his contribution to the " Sabbath Readings " was to misunderstand him. And what a notable chapter could have been added from the source indicated. I have read his *Defence of the Present Patent Law* (1866). It is an able plea, but though it deals with a severely commercial topic in a business-like spirit, the whole pamphlet is lit up by the writer's spiritual personality. Another fact revealed is this: It shows Michael Henry to have been possessed of a ready wit, a keen sense of humor. This note is missing from the volume of *Life Thoughts.*

Even more characteristic is the *Inventor's Almanac,* the annual issue of which was begun in 1858. To comprehend Michael Henry it is absolutely necessary to turn over these sheets, a fine set of which (as continued also by Mr. Ernest de Pass) may be seen in the British Museum. Each *Almanac* consists of a single page, on which are crowded masses of technical information—statistical, practical, and historical. The artistic design is clever. Now, the reason why I am referring to these almanacs is this: From 1862 onwards, the sheets are adorned by quotations as well as pictures. In 1864 Michael Henry quotes from Disraeli: " You have disenthroned force, and placed on her high seat intelligence." Then the compiler must have been struck by the fact that Disraeli's remark had a scriptural analogue. In 1865, and in every subsequent year, the *Almanac* is surmounted by the maxim: " Wisdom is better than strength " (Ecclesiastes). The reference is to chapter 9 verse 16. In 1866 he quotes Gladstone: " There is no honourable, no useful place, upon this busy, teeming earth, for the idle man." In another issue he uses a passage from that once popular versifier Mackay; union had often been tried by man for purposes of war, why not try it for purposes of peace, so that " construction, industry, and mutual aid," may " lead from darkness into light." Naturally enough he revels in Tennyson:

> Men our brothers, men the workers,
> ever reaping something new,
> That which they have done but earnest
> of the things that they shall do.

He used that couplet in 1872. Of course, he presents in due course the same poet's

> Let Knowledge grow from more to more,
> But more of reverence in us dwell!

Quite obvious all this, no doubt. Michael Henry
was, one must admit, given to the cult of the
obvious. Therein lies not blame but praise. Many
of us just fail because we do not see what lies simply before us. Tennyson was the incarnation of
obviousness, hence he helped his generation to see.
Michael Henry had no very keen or far vision.
But he saw straight, he saw true. He was not an
ocean goer, he hugged the shore within a dozen
miles or so. Very like a life-boat, after all!
Clearly a " Michael Henry " in good working order will always be the best monument to his
memory! And he belongs to the type which ought
to be remembered.

THE POEMS OF EMMA LAZARUS

Affixed to the colossal monument, which dominates and ennobles the entrance to New York har-
bor, is, as all the world knows, a poem by Emma
Lazarus (1849-1887). It commemorates her and
her genius. Liberty, " a mighty woman with a
torch," stands there as the " Mother of Exiles,"
crying with silent lips to the older world:

> Give me your tired, your poor,
> Your huddled masses yearning to breathe free,
> The wretched refuse of your teeming shore,
> Send these, the homeless, tempest-tost, to me,
> I lift my lamp beside the golden door.

This sonnet expresses both sides of the writer's
idealism: her devotion to America and her love
for the Jews. She wrote much as a Hellenist, but
her genuine outbursts were stimulated by two
crises: the American War of North and South in
the sixties, and the Russian Persecutions in the
eighties. In a sense it is unfortunate that the May
Laws came so late. Emma Lazarus had but few
years to live after the promulgation of the legislation which sent forth, from their country, those

myriads of Russian Jews, whose presence has so profoundly altered Jewish conditions in various lands. Her Jewish poems are full indeed of fire, but it is the fire of an immature passion. When she died, she had only begun to find herself as the singer of Israel's cause.

Even so, however, her songs will not die. For she realized that Israel is " the slave of the Idea." She did not fully grasp what the Idea was, however. Israel's migrations—including those from Russia to Texas—were all, she felt, towards a destined end, and that end—Freedom:

> Freedom to love the law that Moses brought,
>   To sing the songs of David, and to think
> The thoughts Gabirol to Spinoza taught,
>   Freedom to dig the common earth, to drink
> The universal air—for this they sought
>   Refuge o'er wave and continent, to link
> Egypt with Texas in their mystic chain,
>   And truth's perpetual lamp forbid to wane.

Freedom is part of Israel's Idea; it is not the whole of it.

In her new-found enthusiasm for the Hebrew language she translated much from the medieval poets. But she will always come to one's mind as the bard of Hanukkah. There she comes nearest

EMMA LAZARUS

to the Idea of which Israel is the missioner.
Cheyne, in one of his finest works (*The Origin and
Religious Contents of the Psalter*, pp. 18, 104),
quotes two stanzas from her *Feast of Lights* as an
apt commentary on Psalms 79 and 118, contrasting
the desolation of Zion and the re-dedication:

> They who had camped within the mountain-pass,
>   Couched on the rock, and tented 'neath the sky,
> Who saw from Mizpah's heights the tangled grass
>   Choke the wide Temple-courts, the altar lie
> Disfigured and polluted—who had flung
>   Their faces on the stones, and mourned aloud
> And rent their garments, wailing with one tongue,
>   Crushed as a wind-swept bed of reeds is bowed,
>
> Even they by one voice fired, one heart of flame,
>   Though broken reeds, had risen, and were men,
> They rushed upon the spoiler and o'ercame,
>   Each arm for freedom had the strength of ten.
> Now is their mourning into dancing turned,
>   Their sackcloth doffed for garments of delight,
> Week-long the festive torches shall be burned,
>   Music and revelry wed day with night.

One could quote much else from Emma
Lazarus; her pagan poems written under classic
and romantic influences; her renderings of Heine;
her historical tragedy, the *Dance of Death*, dedi-
cated to George Eliot; her prose epistles, in one of
which occurs her famous use of a Hebrew gram-

matical form. In the Hebrew verb there is an
intensive voice, and so the Jews are the *intensive*
form of any nationality whose language and customs they adopt. Or again, one might cite her
New Ezekiel, her *Bar Kochba,* her *Talmud
Legends,* her *Rashi in Prague,* or, better still, her
lines from Nahum's Spring Song:

> Now the dreary winter's over,
> Fled with him are grief and pain;
> When the trees their bloom recover,
> Then the soul is born again!

But her hand is always firmest when her theme is
the Maccabæan heroism. This subject gave her
the opportunity which her nationalistic mood
needed. We have read part of one of her poems
on the subject, let us read another in full, though it
is perhaps the most familiar of her compositions.
Its title is " The Banner of the Jew." While it
repeats the thought and almost the phrases of the
Feast of Lights, it has more of the lyric lightness
of touch. It runs thus:

> Wake, Israel, wake! Recall to-day
>   The glorious Maccabean rage,
> The sire heroic, hoary-gray,
>   His five-fold lion-lineage:
> The Wise, the Elect, the Help-of-God,
> The Burst-of-Spring, the Avenging Rod.

From Mizpeh's mountain-ridge they saw
  Jerusalem's empty streets, her shrine
Laid waste where Greeks profaned the Law,
  With idol and with pagan sign.
Mourners in tattered black were there,
With ashes sprinkled on their hair.

Then, from the stony peak there rang
  A blast to ope the graves: down poured
The Maccabean clan, who sang
  Their battle-anthem to the Lord.
Five heroes lead, and following, see
Ten thousand rush to victory!

Oh for Jerusalem's trumpet now,
  To blow a blast of shattering power,
To wake the sleepers high and low,
  And rouse them to the urgent hour!
No hand for vengeance—but to save,
A thousand naked swords should wave.

O deem not dead that martial fire,
  Say not the mystic flame is spent!
With Moses' law and David's lyre,
  Your ancient strength remains unbent.
Let but an Ezra rise anew,
To lift the *Banner of the Jew!*

A rag, a mock at first—erelong
  When men have bled and women wept,
To guard its precious folds from wrong,
  Even they who shrunk, even they who slept,
Shall leap to bless it, and to save.
Strike! for the brave revere the brave!

323

This is bold and moving, but the reader cannot fail to observe that the metre and the passion are derived from Byron's *Isles of Greece*. The Hebrew's protest *against* Greece must, forsooth, owe its form and sentiment to the Saxon's plea *for* Greece! The Jewish muse is still in leading strings. The true, full song of Israel's hope is yet to come. None the less, the genius of Emma Lazarus struck truly the key-note to that song. We hear its echo still.

CONDER'S "TENT WORK IN PALESTINE"

He used the Bible too much to please some of the continentals. Compare, for instance, Gautier with Conder. The Frenchman employed the Bible to illustrate the country, the Englishman the country to illustrate the Bible. Which procedure is preferable? The answer is another question. Why does every inch of Palestine interest the modern explorer? No Parthenon is to be seen within its boundaries, no Sphinx. Neither is the Attic beautiful there to charm, nor the Egyptian colossal to provide a thrill. When Thomson (in 1859) called his work "The Land and the Book," he put the seal on the English way of regarding the relation between the geography and the history of the Holy Land. Englishmen have been among the keenest geographers of Palestine because they respond best to its history.

Hence Conder's defect, as some have termed it, is, in truth, his merit. Apart, however, from the pietism of his motives, he deserved well of all who love Palestine. He gave some of his best years to

its survey, and that operation did much to revivify
the country. His services must always have a value
because he, more than any other modern, put an
end to a sort of thing formerly common. I mean
the sort of thing which a pious old dame is said
once to have remarked: " I knew these places were
in the Bible, but I did not know they were in Palestine." Jews in particular owe a good deal to him.
I doubt whether I, for one, would ever have visited
Medyeh—probably Modin, the home of the Mac-
cabæans—but for Conder. I think I could quote by
heart his description how the ancient road from
Jerusalem to Lydda emerged from the rocky Beth-
horon defiles and " ran along a mountain spur
towards the plain "; how, a mile or so to the north
of this main road, the village of Modin was built
upon the southern slopes of the valley; how the
gentle hills of the lowlands (Shephelah) could be
seen from the Modin Knoll, stretching westwards.
" At their feet, amid dark groves of olive, lay the
white town of Lydda, and behind it the broad plain
of Sharon extended to a breadth of ten miles.
Furthest of all, the yellow-gleaming sand-dunes
bounded the rich arable land, and the waters of the
Great Sea (the Mediterranean) shone brightly under the afternoon sun."

This description comes from one of Conder's other books, his *Judas Maccabaeus*. But his earlier *Tent Work in Palestine* (1878) is full of passages just as vivid. It is even more interesting because it shows us the explorer groping for the results, at which he has not yet arrived. Aptly enough, the title-page presents, from a sketch by the author, a theodolite-party at work, for the survey of Western Palestine was conducted on serious trigonometrical methods. That the narrative is so picturesque must not blind us to the truth that the operations were severely scientific. We are now, however, concerned with the pictorial effects. Read, as a parallel to the Modin description, Conder's account of his first visit to Samaria. Taking the north road from Jerusalem, he passes the ranges about Neby Samuel (probably the ancient Mizpah), and sees the hills of Benjamin, "black against a sky of most delicate blush-rose tint, and the contrast was perhaps the finest in a land where fine effects are common at sunset." Then he descends into the rough gorge of the Robbers' Fountain. "The road is not improved by the habit of clearing the stones off the surrounding gardens into the public path." In the east, roads are often thus made the common dumping-ground for rubbish,

and I remember how the walk round the outside of
the Jerusalem walls was much spoilt by the heaps
of vegetable and other refuse which had been flung
over the ramparts. (General Allenby's campaign
has already changed all that for the better.) Pro-
ceeding, " the short twilight gave place to almost
total darkness as we began to climb the watershed
which separates the plain from the valley coming
down from Shiloh, and the moon had risen when
the great shoulder of Gerizim became dimly visible
some ten miles away, with a silvery wreath of cloud
on its summit." The right time to appreciate Palestinian scenes is usually just after sunset. And so,
on this night march, Conder describes how, " creep-
ing beneath the shadow of Gerizim, we gained the
narrow valley of Shechem, and followed a stony
lane between walnut trees under a steep hillside.
The barking of dogs was now heard, and the lights
in camp came into view. My poor terrier was tired
and sleepy, and was set upon at once by Drake's
larger bull-terriers, Jack and Jill, rather a rude
reception after a thirty-mile journey." Mr. C. F.
Tyrwhitt Drake—who died soon afterwards—had
gone on in advance and had placed the camp close
to the beautiful fountain of Ras el-Ain.

Such extended journeys could not be accomplished without paying the price. Thus, after the survey of Samaria, Carmel, and Sharon, operations had to be suspended for a time, simply because the party had reached the limit of endurance. " The fatigue of the campaign had been very great. My eyes were quite pink all over, with the effects of the glare of white chalk, my clothes were in rags, my boots had no soles. The men were no better off, and the horses also were all much exhausted, suffering from soreback, due to the grass diet." But the spirit was stronger than the flesh. " The rest soon restored our energies, and autumn found us once more impatient to be in the fields."

Thence Conder was off to Damascus, Baalbek and Hermon, away from Palestine itself. The ascent of the 9,000 feet of mount Hermon was begun at 10.30 a. m., and at 2 o'clock the summit was reached. But we must pass over the glowing description of the panorama that unfolded itself to the gaze of the explorers. After three months in the north, tents were struck, and the party marched out of their pleasant mountain-camp, bound for Jerusalem and the hills of Judah. Of the many pen-pictures which Conder draws, we will stay only to regard one—the description of Bethar, where

Bar Cochba made his great effort at recovering Jewish independence (about the year 135 of the present era). Conder locates the fortress at the modern village Bittîr (at which there is now a railway station). It is about thirty-five miles from the sea, and about five from Jerusalem. "On every side, except the south, it is surrounded by deep and rugged gorges, and it is supplied with fresh water from a spring above the village. On the north the position would have been impregnable, as steep cliffs rise from the bottom of the ravine, upon which the houses are perched. The name (Bittîr) exactly represents the Hebrew (Bethar), and the distances agree with those noticed by Eusebius and the Talmud. Nor must the curious title be forgotten, which is applied to a shapeless mass of ruin on the hill, immediately west of Bittîr, for the name Khurbet el Yehûd—Ruin of the Jews—may be well thought to hand down traditionally among the natives of the neighbourhood the memory of the great catastrophe of Bethar." Whether this place is the true site of Bar Cochba's Bethar may be seriously questioned, but no other view can claim to be more certain. "The site of Bethar must still be considered doubtful," says that good authority, S. Krauss, who himself is inclined to the theory which places the fortress much further north, near Sepphoris.

We should like to linger over the rest of Conder's journey, but the few lines that remain must be devoted to his final remarks. Conder, it must ever be remembered, was one of the first to dispute the then current belief that the Holy Land had lost its old character for fertility, and that changes in climate had induced an irreparable barrenness. He maintained in particular that the supposed dearth of water had been much exaggerated by recent tourists. " With respect to the annual rainfall, it is only necessary to note that, with the old cisterns cleaned and mended, and the beautiful tanks and aqueducts repaired, the ordinary fall would be quite sufficient for the wants of the inhabitants and for irrigation." (Here, too, recent events have effected an agreeable transformation.) And, in general " the change in productiveness which has really occurred in Palestine, is due to decay of cultivation, to decrease of population, and to bad government. It is Man and not Nature, who has ruined the good land in which was ' no lack,' and it is, therefore, within the power of human industry to restore the old country to its old condition of agricultural prosperity." Construct roads, raise irrigation works, promote afforestation—those were the measures Conder suggested, after the three strenuous years of his survey (1872 to 1875). Such optimistic opinions are now quite common; and, we may hope, are tending towards realization, if only men's hopes are not set too high. But let us not forget that among the first moderns to formulate such opinions, on the basis of *exact knowledge,* was the author of *Tent Work in Palestine.*

KALISCH'S " PATH AND GOAL "

Of Marcus Kalisch's learned commentaries on the Bible it has been truly said that they are a thorough summary of all that had been written on the subject up to the date when those commentaries were published. He not only knew everything, but he had assimilated it. Nor was it only his learning that placed him among the first among the Jewish scholars of the second part of the nineteenth century. He was original as well; that he " anticipated Wellhausen," more than one has declared of him, as they have declared of others before Kalisch.

Learning and originality make a fairly strong instrument for drawing out the truth. But another strand is needed to compose the threefold cord that shall not easily be broken. This, too, Kalisch had at his command. It is the strand of sentiment. In his more orthodox days when he produced his *Exodus* (1855), and in his more rationalistic period when he gave to the world his *Balaam* and his *Jonah* (1887-8)—at all stages of his activity he was never the mere philologist. Like Sheridan's character, he was a man of sentiment; but unlike Joseph Surface, his sentiment was genuine. He was, to put the same truth in other words, an expounder of ideas as well as a critic of words.

It should have surprised no one to meet Kalisch in any situation where the qualities above defined could be exercised. Yet some of those who only thought of him as the Hebrew grammarian must have opened their eyes when the fact was brought to their notice that within a couple of years of printing his *Genesis* (1858) he issued a small volume on Oliver Goldsmith. In 1860 he spoke the substance of this volume as " two lectures delivered to a village audience." The theme was treated by him with considerable learning, but with an even more considerable good feeling. I remember particularly two or three sentences in this book. " Forgive his faults, but do not forget them " is one—I quote from memory and may not be verbally exact. Forgiveness not only differs from forgetfulness, but, humanely considered, the two things are scarcely consistent. You really can only forgive when you remember—all that the man was whom you are judging. Another sentence that I recall is this: " You will find Goldsmith's life again in his writings, and his writings in his life." This is a notable conception, not original to Kalisch. But the turn he gives to it seems to me quite fresh.

Goldsmith, he asserts, was a great writer and—
despite the faults aforementioned—a good man.
"You see his goodness in his writings and his
greatness in his life"—a brilliant epigram, but also
a neat description of the ideal man of letters.

But how came it that Marcus Kalisch, a German
and a Jew, was addressing village audiences in
England at all? Born in Pomerania in 1828, he
had come to England fresh from the Universities
of Berlin and Halle. Like so many others of various nationalities and creeds, he had played a generous part in the 1848 affair, and felt unsafe after
its suppression. Nathan Marcus Adler had settled in London in 1845. The refugee found an
asylum with the new chief rabbi: Kalisch served
the latter as secretary for five years. His former
employer must have felt fairly uncomfortable when
Kalisch's *Leviticus* appeared (1867-72), for this
was a pretty thorough departure from the old-
fashioned standpoint. Kalisch, of course, was not
without honor in his own community. He had a
real, though not an undiscriminating, admirer in
the late A. L. Green. We still, however, seem
rather far off from solving the riddle: how came
Kalisch to be talking to English village audiences
on Oliver Goldsmith or on any other subject? The

answer is given with the names of the villages. They were Aston Clinton and Mentmore in the county of Buckinghamshire—places long associated with the country homes of the Rothschilds. In 1853 Kalisch was appointed tutor to the sons of Baron Lionel de Rothschild. From that date until Kalisch's death, in 1885, there was no break in the cordial relations between the Rothschilds and the scholar. They provided the leisure, and he provided the capacity to make worthy use of it. Countless are the honorable incidents in the Rothschild record, but there is none on which a Jewish writer more loves to dwell than on the association of the family with the author of *Path and Goal.*

The scene of that work is Cordova Lodge, the house of Gabriel de Mondoza, situated in one of the northern suburbs of London. It was " an unpretending structure of moderate dimensions, but adorned with consummate taste and judgment." The further description of the house rather reminds one of Disraeli's creations. And this Lodge, " a veritable rus in urbe," with its Greek busts and "modest conservatories "—there is not lacking even " a diminutive farm "—was, we are told, so located and ordered as to afford " an atmosphere of calm cheerfulness, inviting the mind at once to concentration and intercommunion." The owner, in whose abode Kalisch represents his characters as gathered, was descended from a distinguished family of Spanish Jews, who had come from Holland to England during Cromwell's protectorate. His mother was a German, " of an essentially artistic nature." From his father he derived his love for the Bible, from his mother his admiration for the Classics; and doubtful as to which to prefer, " he clung the more firmly to both, and laboured to weld the conceptions of the Scriptures and of Hellenism into one homogeneous design."

His house was the habitual meeting-place for many native and foreign guests, and during the International Exhibition a specially representative group are found at Cordova Lodge, conducting a " discussion of the elements of civilisation and the conditions of happiness." This discussion is the substance of the volume entitled *Path and Goal.* Such symposia go back to Plato, but it was W. H. Mallock who, with his *New Republic,* re-popularized the genre in England. This appeared in 1877; Kalisch's *Path and Goal* followed it in 1880. The disputants in the latter work include Christians of all degrees of high and low Churchiness; a naturalist and a Hellenist; a Reform and an Orthodox

Rabbi; a Parsee and a Mohammedan; a Brahman and a Buddhist. Perhaps the most remarkable feature of this gathering is Kalisch's recognition of the importance of the Eastern religions. Sometimes, indeed, those who try to prefigure the future of the world's religion take account of Islam. But very few remember the beliefs and institutions of India. The learning with which Kalisch discusses the Indian systems would be amazing were one not prepared for it by previous knowledge of his encyclopedic acquirements.

We will not follow out into any detail the course of the conversations at Cordova Lodge. It is cleverly constructed, being based on a discussion of Ecclesiastes. The whole of that biblical book appears in the second chapter of *Path and Goal,* and it is the text for what follows. What is the object of the interchange of these opinions? " We do not search for that which appertains to *one* time or to *one* nation, but those truths which flow from the constitution and wants of human nature, and are on that account universal and unchanging." No definite result is reached, except, perhaps, the final justification of Mondoza's suggested " eucrasy "— the " harmony of character which is the perfection of culture." Here, then, we have the very antithesis to the view expressed in Herzberg's *Jewish Family Papers*. Kalisch believed in the possible harmonization of various elements into a perfect culture. But he does not describe as Jewish the resultant harmony. He would not have cared at all about the name; he was chiefly concerned with the thing. And in the light of this—for I think we may not unjustly attribute the host's sentiments to the host's author—he regarded the " political community as only an elementary stage "; nationality was at best preparatory for the " universal union " of men; while " the feeling of nationality is a onesidedness to be merged in a genuine and ardent cosmopolitanism." Cosmopolitanism is the political correlative to a belief in culture. In the end there is a very general agreement among the visitors at Cordova Lodge. " Is this a dream? " cries Mondoza. " It heralds," said Rabbi Gideon, with a trembling voice, " the approach of the time predicted by our prophets, when ' the Lord shall be One and His name One '; and when ' He shall bless the nations saying, Blessed be Egypt My people, and Assyria the work of My hands, and Israel Mine inheritance.' " (Isaiah 19. 25.) So, after all, Kalisch's " Goal " is not widely distant from the Goal that may rightly be termed Jewish.

FRANZ DELITZSCH'S "IRIS"

Light and color are the themes of the poet. But they and the flowers attract the theologian also. Franz Delitzsch produced his *Studies in Color and Talks on Flowers* in 1888 (an English version appearing in the following year). The book gives the lie to the supposition that the technical scholar is so engaged in dissecting things of beauty, that he is blind to the beauty of things. Delitzsch—the student and interpreter of the Bible—assures us that he could not remember the time when he did not muse on the language of colors; while, as for flowers, they ever had heavenly things to tell him; in their perfume he felt " the nearness and breath of the Creator." Hence he called his book *Iris*. " The prismatic colours of the rainbow, the brilliant sword-lily, that wonderful part of the eye which gives it its colour, and the messenger of heaven who beams with joy, youth, beauty, and love, are all called *Iris*." A pretty notion, this, so to name a book which is occupied largely with the lore of Bible and Talmud.

But the question arises: Did the olden Hebrews and their rabbinic descendants appreciate colors?

Here we are face to face with a basic error to which
some investigators have succumbed. They rely
too much on *words*. The Hebrew names for
colors are vague and few. Does it, however, follow that the ancient people were unable to enjoy
the blue of the sky because they had no word for
sky-blue? Men do not *name* everything they *know*.
There is, for instance, no specific Hebrew for
volcano, yet there are a score of passages in which
volcanic phenomena are forcibly described in the
Old Testament. Delitzsch did not belong to the
superficial theorists just cited. He points out that,
though biblical language has no adjective for blue,
it compares the sky to sapphire in the Sinaitic
theophany (Exodus 24. 10), as well as in Ezekiel's
vision of the divine throne. " Sapphire-blue is the
blue of heaven; the colour of the atmosphere as
illumined by the sun, through which shine the dark
depths of space, the colour of the finite pervaded
by the infinite, the colour taken by that which is
most heavenly as it comes down to the earthly, the
colour of the covenant between God and man."
So, too, the Midrash says of the blue fringe worn
by Israelites on the corners of their garments—
a blue of the purple hyacinth hue—that it was
reminiscent of the heavens and the Throne of

341

Glory. And blue, continues Delitzsch, passes almost universally as the color of fidelity. He proves this by reference to German and Sanskrit. The Indians would say of a steadfast man that he was " as unchangeable as the indigo flower," which is as durable as it is lovely. " But in biblical symbolism there is associated with blue the idea of the blue sky, and with the blue sky the idea of the Godhead coming forth from its mysterious dwelling in the unseen world, and graciously condescending to the creature." Delitzsch, scientific commentator though he was, had something of the *darshan* in him, and that accounts in part for his charm. The spirit of Midrash rests where it will: it is a happy truth that it sometimes finds itself a home in the hearts of others besides the sons of Israel.

Delitzsch, then, may be likened to the *darshan*: he is equally at home as allegorist. He can use the method of an Abbahu; he can also follow the manner of a Philo. Take, for example, his treatment of the four colors which are found in the priestly vestments—purple-red, purple-blue, scarlet, and white. White, he says, is the sacred color. Light is white and God is white. Dressed in the white of holiness, the priests blessed Israel in the words: " May the Lord make His face shine in light upon

342

thee." Delitzsch interprets light in the sense of love. This is not quite adequate. He often quotes German university customs in illustration of his views; it is a pity that he forgot the motto of the University of Oxford, *Dominus illuminatio mea* (" the Lord is my light "), from the first verse of the twenty-seventh Psalm. " God is the author of knowledge as well as the source of love," comments Mr. C. G. Montefiore. White would stand for mind-service as well as heart-service: illumination, no doubt, is emotional, but it must also be intellectual to be sane and complete. Scarlet, on the other hand, continues Delitzsch in his allegory of the priestly colors, is the contrast to white. Isaiah speaks of sin " red as scarlet "—scarlet is the color of fire, hence of sin and the anger it evokes. " Scarlet with white in the dress of the high priest, therefore, means that he is the servant of that God who is holy not only in His love, but also in His anger." A fine phrase that, showing deep insight into the Hebrew conception of God. Delitzsch, obviously, is not to be lumped together with those who would make of God all love; there is a holy anger, too, which belongs (inseparably with the love) to the divine nature. With regard to the two purples in the priestly robes, they typify majesty, for the dye was costly and its effects magnificent. Purple-red points to " God's majesty as the exalted One, and purple-blue to God's majesty in His condescension. " For," continues Delitzsch, " even taken in itself, the impression produced by purple-red is severe and earnest: whereas purple-blue has a soft tranquillizing effect. And whereas purple-red suggests the God of judgment who, when He frowns in anger, changes the heavens into blackness and the moon into blood, purple-blue suggests the God of peace, who overarches the earth with the blue of heaven, like a tent of peace." How very fanciful, but how very Philonean, and therefore how very Jewish all this is!

There is much more as good as this in *Iris*. For instance, one would hardly have looked for poetry in the laws of *bedikah*—the minute scrutiny of the carcasses of animals as regards symptoms of disease. But just as in Samson's riddle out of the body of the lion there came forth sweetness, so in *Iris* the author extracts aesthetics from the *bedikah* rules, and sees in them evidence of the close observation of colors by the rabbinic legalists. " The colour of the lung especially is subjected to the most careful examination. It is reckoned healthy if it is black like the Eastern eye paint—that is, tending to blueish—or green like leek, or red, or liver-coloured, but it is declared to be unsuitable for eating if the colour is as black as ink, yellowish-green like hops, yellow like the yolk of an egg, yellow like saffron, yellow-red like raw flesh." And after the recital, Delitzsch exclaims: " Is not this a rich variegated sampler of colours? "

Since the date when Delitzsch wrote there has come about an important change in the opinion of anthropologists. Little more than a quarter of a century has passed, but all anthropological theorists no longer accept (though some still do) one theory on which Delitzsch builds, namely, that primitive peoples were color-blind. Several eminent authorities deny that savages lack the power to discriminate colors. The fact simply is that with advance in culture there enters greater precision in *nomenclature;* color-language becomes not so much more definite, as of wider range. But why? Surely not because of more accurate observation of natural tints. Culture associates itself with town life, and urbans are far more color-blind than rustics. At least, statistics are said to prove this, though Dr. Maurice Fishberg questions one of the inferences. The discussion has importance owing to the statement often made that Jews are more subject to color-blindness than Gentiles, the suggestion being that, as Jews live predominatingly in towns, they see less *green* than do those who dwell in the country. Dr. Fishberg, on the other hand, maintains that, while the poor and ill-nourished are always susceptible to color-blindness, Jews of the well-nourished classes are quite as good distinguishers of shades of color as the rest of the population of the same social status.

There remains something else to add. Culture carries with it luxury, and luxury leads to the manufacture of silks and cloths of every variety of shade. It is the mediæval improvement in the *art of dyeing* that has produced the increase of definition and range in the color vocabulary. And the art of dyeing owed much to Jews. To repeat a well-known fact, wherever he went on his Itinerary in the mid-twelfth century, Benjamin of Tudela always found Jewish dyers. Here, however, we must break off, for we seem getting a longish way from *Iris*. But not really. The book itself makes no attempt to be systematic, and discursiveness is, accordingly, not inappropriate in a *causerie* on Franz Delitzsch's masterpiece.

"THE PRONAOS" OF I. M. WISE

Of Isaac Mayer Wise it is customary to speak as an organizer and nothing more. True, the most significant performance of his long life (1819-1900) was the foundation of institutions for American Reform Judaism. More than any other leader of his age he realized two ideas which are usually regarded as contradictory, but which Wise saw can and must be harmonized. The two ideas are not of equal importance. The basis of a sound Jewish life is the recognition of the congregation as the unit. Wise perceived this, but he also saw that some sort of grouping of the units is necessary to convert the congregations into a community. This he effected by founding the Hebrew Union College as representative of the Union of American Hebrew Congregations. The Union devised by Wise differs essentially from the United Synagogue of London. The latter depends on the principle of control, the former on the principle of co-operation. This is not the place to discuss the relative values of the two principles. Suffice it to indicate the distinction.

Yet, though Wise owes to his organizing skill his fame as " the most potent factor in the history of Judaism in America," he was also an author. His contributions to literature were many and varied. He was, above all, an energetic journalist; but he was a novelist and a dramatist as well. A careful study of his writings on religion will convince any unprejudiced reader that Wise was also a theologian of no mean order. In his life-time it was customary to throw easy jibes at him as an ignoramus. But the charge was false. Not long ago I read for the first time Wise's most ambitious books, as well as the *Selected Writings,* edited in 1900 by Drs. Philipson and Grossman. Now Wise, throughout his career, worked consciously with the " aim to reconcile Judaism with the age and its needs." Every Jewish leader, to whatever school he belongs, does that. With Wise, however, the aim was most consciously felt. Hence his writings were all directed to current problems, to the fashions of the hour; and as a result his books seemed ephemeral. But the strange thing is that, when the fashions have passed, it is seen that the treatment of them has permanent worth. I have been again and again struck by Wise's learning and originality. He was a pioneer, for instance, in his treatment of Christianity. He held the fantastic theory that Paul was identical with Elisha ben

ISAAC MAYER WISE

Abuyah, and in other points displays a somewhat perverse ingenuity. But he was a pioneer in trying to separate the supernatural from the natural in the records of the early church. " The God Jesus," he said, " and the supernatural Paul appear small in the focus of reason. The patriotic and enthusiastic Jesus, and the brave, bold, wise Paul are grand types of humanity." The epithets applied by Wise are not all well chosen; there is frequently an eccentricity in Wise's characterizations. But the main distinction which he draws is sound. Again, Wise was a pioneer not so much in laying stress on the prophetic Judaism, because Geiger did the same before him; but where Wise led was in his effort to attach the prophetic ideals to the congregational life. He understood that " social service " ought to be an integral element in every synagogue's activity. " Whatever a congregation does, it must never neglect the first of all its duties—the Messianic duty of Israel. It must contribute its full share to the elevation of human nature, the redemption of mankind, the sovereignty of truth, and the supremacy of reason, freedom, and virtue."

Wise, however, refused to set the Prophets above the Law. The " Revelation on Mount Sinai " was for him " valid eternally." It is because of this aspect of his work that I have chosen his *Pronaos* as the peg on which to hang these thoughts. The book appeared in Cincinnati in 1891, and its full title is " Pronaos to Holy Writ establishing, on documentary evidence, the authorship, date, form, and contents of each of its books, and the Authenticity of the Pentateuch." The book is among the earliest of the reasoned replies to the Higher Criticism. Wise would have nothing to do with the modern treatment of the Pentateuch. He had as little patience with Graetz as he had with Wellhausen. The Pentateuch is through and through Mosaic. Moses wrote Genesis and Deuteronomy with his own hands; the rest was set down soon after his death from the records which he had left for the purpose. And further: " There exists no solid ground on which to base any doubt in the authenticity of any book of Holy Writ." With that emphatic assertion the book ends.

Wise, it must be confessed, seemed unaware of the constructive side of criticism. To him criticism seemed entirely negative. Again, he was unable to see that the value of the Bible may continue, even though the older conception of authenticity be modified. But the interest of his *Pronaos* just lies in the vigor with which he maintains that older conception.

His defence is spirited, and in many ways convincing. Criticism was undoubtedly wrong when it treated Judaism as the creation of the prophets, and the Pentateuch as lower in worth than Micah and Isaiah. I do not remember that any predecessor of Wise so thoroughly employed the argument of *continuity*. There is, he said, an "uninterrupted tradition," the whole is " a logical organism," every part in its right place, fulfilling its due function. Now this is the real justification of the Bible. There are variations in the points of view of various inspired writers, but the whole tendency is one, there is consistency of purpose. Wise deserves lasting gratitude for urging this truth so powerfully. Well might he term his book a *Pronaos,* a " door leading into the interior of the sanctuary." For a detail, it is significant to find that Wise anticipated the newer, though I think erratic, direction of criticism in our day. He absolutely refused to admit that the different names applied to God (Adonai and Elohim) point to different authors or ages.

Differ though we may with Wise—some of us on account of his rejection of criticism, others because of his elevation of " Mosaism " into a cult, others again because of both of these things—it is

351

not possible to withhold from him the crown of scholarship. In particular, his *Pronaos* abounds in acute and fresh contributions to the biblical problem. It is, moreover, a striking instance of the ironies of controversy that the most orthodox book on the Pentateuch was written by the leader of American reform! Cincinnati, under the influence of Wise, was certainly much more conservative in biblical exegesis than Breslau was under the influence of Graetz. If in the seventies and eighties a student had desired to work in an environment which acknowledged the older views of biblical inspiration, he would have found himself more at home in the Hebrew Union College than in the Frankel Seminary. In the course of this series of papers, several anomalies have been discussed. But none of them is more remarkable than the contrast between Wise and Graetz. There is another side to it, of course. Graetz took a wider view of tradition than did Wise, who never truly grasped the meaning of tradition. Yet the fact remains that in so far as the question of a tradition concerns the Bible, Wise stood far more firmly in the old paths than did many who pass for champions of tradition.

A BAEDEKER LITANY

In the Baedeker Handbook for Palestine and Syria there is a well-known description of the scene at the western wall of the temple. In A. and C. Black's Guide to Jerusalem, the Wailing Place is included among " Minor Sights," but Baedeker *stars* it, thus giving it a testimonial of importance. Not being an inn, the wall could spare this mark. I remember reading a clever story called " The Lost Star." A visitor to a hotel was dissatisfied with his treatment, and his complaints to the manager were impatiently received. When the guest departed, he simply said: " I am Baedeker. You have lost your star." The Wailing Place could do without Baedeker's patronage.

Now, it is not my purpose to discuss the history of praying at the temple wall. Jerome, in the fourth century, speaks pathetically of the Jews " buying their tears," paying for the privilege of weeping by the wall on the anniversary of the temple's destruction. But what will concern us now is Baedeker's account of the liturgy used at the prayers. The Rev. W. T. Gidney (as quoted in Black) asserts that there is used " a kind of liturgy," the concluding part of which is:

> Lord, build; Lord build—
> Build Thy house speedily.
> In haste! in haste! even in our days.
> Build Thy house speedily.
> In haste! in haste! even in our days,
> Build Thy house speedily.

I do not know whether any Jews actually sing this Passover hymn (*Addir hu*) on other occasions during the year. Murray's Palestine Handbook asserts that "the lamentations are taken from the 79th Psalm," a statement which points to the same source as that relied on by Baedeker. The latter gives two forms, of which the first runs thus:

Leader: For the palace that lies desolate:
Response: We sit in solitude and mourn.

Leader: For the palace that is destroyed:
Response: We sit, etc.

Leader: For the walls that are overthrown:
Response: We sit, etc.

Leader: For our majesty that is departed:
Response: We sit, etc.

Leader: For our great men who lie dead:
Response: We sit, etc.

Leader: For the precious stones that are burned:
Response: We sit, etc.

Leader: For the priests who have stumbled:
Response: We sit, etc.

Leader: For our kings who have despised Him:
Response: We sit, etc.

Whence did the compiler of Bacdeker derive this? From the Karaites. If one turns to the fourth volume of the Karaite liturgy, published in Vienna in 1854, page 208, this litany is to be found. It is part of a very long series of prayers (which include, on page 212, the passage which, in Baedeker, follows the one cited above). Psalm 79, referred to in Murray, appears in the same Karaite book on page 206. The selections are a tiny fraction of the whole. The Karaite prayers are always extremely long. Thus, their marriage service fills eleven large, closely printed sides. The Jerusalem prayers are even more elaborate. As the pilgrim starts from home for the Holy City, the congregation turns out to give him a send off, reciting *sixteen* Psalms as a supplication for his protection, and other *fourteen* Psalms in praise of Jerusalem. He then proceeds on his way. When he arrives at the city, as far off as the distance at which a man can recognize his fellow, he rends his garments and mourns as for a lost first-born. He then recites parts of the Lamentations, and enough Psalms and

Selihot to occupy another ten pages. Some of us complain of the length of our prayers; when we look at the weary mass of the Karaite liturgy, we stand amazed at our own moderation.

Having tracked Baedeker to his source, and restricting ourselves to the pages from which he quotes, it is worth comparing his version with the original. The omissions made are so serious as to spoil the beauty of the whole, for beautiful it assuredly is of its kind. The fault arises from Baedeker only reading down one of the two columns. Now the lines are alphabetical, and must be read across, not down the page. There are other faults; for instance *palace* in the second line is a mistake for *house,* but the compiler may have used a slightly different version. In the one before me there is nothing to correspond to *For our great men who lie dead.* The rest of the lines are the same as in the book I am using. But note how the effect suffers by the loss of the half-lines to which I have referred. Thus Baedeker gives *For the priests who have stumbled,* but omits the complementary phrase *For our studies which were interrupted.* Again, Baedeker quotes *For the precious stones which are burned,* but fails to follow it up with *For loving ones that were separated,* a fine line which ought to have been retained in any abbreviation, however short.

The only other passage quoted in Baedeker, " another antiphon " or responsive chant, is the following:

Leader: We pray Thee, have mercy on Zion!
Response: Gather the children of Jerusalem.

Leader: Haste, haste, Redeemer of Zion!
Response: Speak to the heart of Jerusalem.

Leader: May beauty and majesty surround Zion!
Response: Ah! turn Thyself mercifully to Jerusalem.

Leader: May the kingdom soon return to Zion!
Response: Comfort those who mourn over Jerusalem.

Leader: May peace and joy abide with Zion!
Response: And the branch (of Jesse) spring up in Jerusalem.

Comparing this with the Hebrew original, there is no such mistake as in the previous case. The summarizer has correctly read the lines across the page. There are certain slips, and more than a half of the whole (which again runs in alphabetical sequence) is left out; but the shortening is here no loss, as the best lines have been selected.

Besides these prayers, the Karaite book includes a large number of hymns. Among them, inappropriately enough, is the piyyut on the offering of Isaac. In the Sephardic service this properly belongs to the New Year; it goes to a swinging melody at Bevis Marks. True, the scene was Moriah, the temple hill. But the Karaite book gives no direction that the shofar is to be sounded. None the less, it finishes this piyyut with the prayer that God will hearken to the shofar sounds and say unto Zion: " The time of salvation has come." Obviously, this is a fitting prelude to the blowing of the shofar on Rosh ha-Shanah. But it has no right where this Karaite book has transplanted it, although the bulk of the hymn suits well enough the liturgy of the Wailing Place.

IMBER'S SONG

Throughout its whole range modern Hebrew literature can offer no poem to rival in popularity Imber's song. Naphtali Herz Imber was born in 1856, and wrote *Ha-Tikwah* in his youth in one of his many moods. His disposition was wayward; he had a full share of the artistic self-consciousness. Some of his characteristics are accurately hit off in Melchitsedek Pinchas of Mr. Zangwill's *Children of the Ghetto*.

Ha-Tikwah owes its fame to the directness of its sentiment. What makes for weakness in it as a poem makes for strength in it as a song. The most effective national hymns are not usually the most poetical. " God save the King " is doggerel; " Rule Britannia " is bombast. But both put patriotic thoughts in straightforward terms, both are happily wedded to simple tunes within the range of average voices. *Ha-Tikwah* satisfies both these tests. The melody is beautiful and easily sung by large masses of people. The opening line of Imber's refrain: " Our hope has not perished yet " is certainly derived from the National Song, " Poland has not perished yet," to which the Polish legions marched. So the melody of *Ha-Tikwah* is said to be a Polish folk-tune, but it closely resembles a favorite melody of the Sephardim. Various settings of the tune differ in detail, and the same is true of the current versions of Imber's words. It is strange that the versions—all known to me—retain unanimously the ungrammatical second stanza. It would, I admit, be difficult to correct it without destroying the rhythm, and poetical license has worse things to answer for. Indeed the grammatical lapse, to which I refer, is regarded by some authorities as perfectly normal and admissible in the new Hebrew.

The power of *Ha-Tikwah,* as has just been said, arises from its directness. There is no subtlety in its thought, no changes through its nine verses. Just as few ever sing through " God Save the King," so few sing all the verses of *Ha-Tikwah.* The stanzas tend to become monotonous. They all say the same thing; and it is not surprising that the number of verses is curtailed in some printed editions (thus in Idelsohn five of the nine verses complete the song). The burden of all the verses is identical. The hope of a return to the land of Israel will never die, so long as this or that endures. Each verse adds a this or a that to the count. While myriads of Jews go as pilgrims to the sepulchres of

NAPHTALI HERZ IMBER

the fathers, while a single eye is left to drop its
tear over the ruins of the temple, while the waters
of the Jordan swell between its banks and fall with
a rush through the sea of Kinnereth, while a drop
of blood courses through a Jewish vein, while Israel
retains his national aspirations, still may he hope
for their fulfilment. Some of these appeals are
genuinely pathetic, and the final appeal is magnificent in its strength. Only with the end of the Jews
will come the end of the hope. This is the only
way to write a popular song. There must be no
nuances, but just a confident assertion. Imber supplies exactly that; nothing less, and nothing more.

Nothing more, for the song is not in any sense a
declaration of the end. It deals only with the
means, making them into an end. Unquenchable,
he cries, is the hope of a return; no one has expressed this hope more vigorously and takingly.
But what is to be the result of the return? With
what ideals are the patriots filled? *Ha-Tikwah*
is silent on these questions. Imber was not qualified to reply to them. He had no depth of spiritual
feeling, and though he was capable of inspiriting,
he was incapable of inspiring. Hence the absence
of all Messianic thought in *Ha-Tikwah*. Compare it, for instance, with *Leka Dodi;* the Friday

night hymn is like *Ha-Tikwah,* a song of the return, but, unlike *Ha-Tikwah,* it is Messianic, and is also a song of the rebuilding. When the history of the neo-Zionist movement comes to be written, this fact will undoubtedly come into due prominence: namely, that we have been passing through a phase in which the hope of the return has been divorced from the hope of the rebuilding.

It is remarkable that some versions of the refrain remove the only words which possibly can bear a Messianic construction. I have not before me the original words of Imber himself, and I have a notion that Mr. David Yellin is responsible in part for the chorus. Be that as it may, in the last line Jerusalem is described as " the city where David encamped." The phrase comes from the opening line of the twenty-ninth chapter of Isaiah. " Woe to Ariel, Ariel, city where David encamped "—Ariel is either " Lion of God " or, as the Targum takes it, " Altar-hearth." The Rabbis combined both senses. Ariel was the altar, yet they saw something lion-shaped in the sanctuary. In Isaiah the passage is one of doom, Ariel is to be humiliated by the Assyrians. Curiously enough, the ancient Greek translation gives also a hostile turn to the words " city where David encamped," rendering " against which David encamped." But this is erroneous. The meaning is: the city in which David dwelt, selecting it as the royal capital. David, it is true, did not build the temple, but he brought the ark thither, and offered sacrifices on the occasion, and later on built an altar. Not only, then, is Ariel justly to be termed the city where David encamped, but the use of the phrase in *Ha-Tikwah* supplies the missing Messianic hope, for David is the type of this hope. In the version of *Ha-Tikwah* printed by Idelsohn four verses are omitted, and some of those which are retained are set in an inverted order. More culpably, the refrain is weakened into " the city of Zion and Jerusalem," thus removing the Davidic touch. The change does not merely offend against reason; it also sins against rhyme; thus adding another instance to many others of the destructive tamperings with masterpieces which some editors seem unable to avoid.

One other striking merit of *Ha-Tikwah* must be observed. Unlike many other poets of Zion, Imber does not denounce. He makes no attack on those who do not share his feelings. He points to the continued existence of the hope for the return, but he refrains from condemning, except by the merest implication, those who have no consciousness of the hope. There is true art here, which I am able to appreciate, far removed as I am from Imber's nationalism. For, on the one hand, art is best when it pleases some without paining others. Imber pleases those who agree with him without paining the rest. On the other hand, art is strongest when it does not recognize that there are others to be displeased. The confident note is the artistic note. The poet assumes that what he feels is the only thing to feel. To talk of doubters is to throw doubt on himself. A popular song cannot stoop to argument. It is categorical. Thus Imber's *Ha-Tikwah* can be enjoyed by those who do not accept its message. And its melody is sung at table, to Psalm 126, by some who never sing the tune to Imber's words. " When the Lord turned again the captivity of Zion, we were like unto them that dream. Then was our mouth filled with laughter, and our tongue with exultation; then said they among the nations: The Lord hath done great things for them." Psalm 126, when all is said and done, is the most exquisite Song of the Return ever written. " They that sow in tears shall reap in joy." We can all realize the pathos and the hope, even though we are not at one as to the nature of the harvest that is to be reaped.

INDEX

INDEX

INDEX

INDEX

Vogelstein, 62.
Voltaire, 109, 175, 303.
Vossius, Isaac, 147, 149.

Wagenseil, 288.
Walker, George, 191-198.
Walker's *Theodore Cyphon*, 191-198.
Wellhausen, Julius, 186, 333, 350.
Wendland, 26.
Wharton, Edith, 112.
Whewell's *Astronomy*, 222.
White, Joseph Blanco, 220-225.
Williamson, 154.

Wise, Isaac Mayer, 347-352.
Wolf, Lucien, 226.
Wordsworth, William, 166.

Yellin, David, 362.
Yellin method, the, 248.
Yosif Omez, by Joseph Hahn, 129-135.

Zangwill, Israel, 80, 88, 228, 240, 359.
Zedner, J., 103.
Zunz, Leopold, 97, 98, 102, 116, 118, 119, 120, 254.

𝕿𝖍𝖊 𝕷𝖔𝖗𝖉 𝕭𝖆𝖑𝖙𝖎𝖒𝖔𝖗𝖊 𝕻𝖗𝖊𝖘𝖘
BALTIMORE, MD., U. S. A.